500

sushi

500

sushi

the only sushi compendium you'll ever need

Caroline Bennett
with Hong Sui Li & Sami Nkaili

APPLE

A Quintet Book

First published in the UK in 2012 by
Apple Press
7 Greenland Street
London NW1 0ND
United Kingdom

www.apple-press.com

ISBN: 978-1-84543-477-9
QTT.FSUS

This book was conceived, designed, and produced by
Quintet Publishing Limited
6 Blundell Street
London N7 9BH
United Kingdom

Chefs/Food Stylists: Hong Sui Li and Sami Nkaili
Photographer: Ian Garlick
Art Director: Michael Charles
Project Editor: Ross Fulton
Editorial Director: Donna Gregory
Publisher: Mark Searle

10 9 8 7 6 5 4 3 2 1

Printed in China by 1010 Printing International Ltd.

contents

introduction 6

basic recipes 26

nigiri sushi 56

gunkan battleship sushi 92

hosomaki 122

futomaki 144

sashimi 188

temaki hand roll 220

chirashi, onigiri & pressed sushi 246

index 282

introduction

Say 'Japanese food' to almost anyone and the chances are they will say 'sushi'. From Seoul to New York via Munich and Madrid, it is Japan's most famous culinary export. Perhaps this is because sushi is synonymous with the traditions and culture of Japan in so many ways. Japan is an island country surrounded by seas that are abundant with a huge variety of fish. Its land mass is relatively small, and much of that is given over to rice cultivation; the steep slopes of the Japanese Alps don't allow for large arable stretches of land. Thus a national dish based on the nutrition available in fish and rice was inevitable. As well, from an aesthetic point of view, sushi is the embodiment of Zen principles of minimalism, reflection of nature, harmony and balance.

We usually rely very heavily on our sense of smell, more so even than our sense of taste, to appreciate food. Sushi, being cold, has very little aroma, so must rely wholly upon the taste buds being stimulated by appearance.

My first experience of eating sushi was just that; I saw a beautifully colourful and artful lacquerware bowl full of exquisitely presented sushi and was immediately drawn to it. Whilst my first taste of sushi wasn't unpleasant, neither did it immediately jump out at me. It was a couple of weeks later that I realised I was hankering for it. That was really it. From that second time forward, I was hooked. And therein lies a third point – the understated nature of all things beautiful and delicious in Japan.

This notion is embodied in the ideal of wabi sabi, the essence of Japanese aesthetic, which seeks to appreciate the whole of something being greater than the sum of its parts. Wabi sabi is a state of consciousness. Its beauty hidden in the aesthetic or feeling experienced between you and something in the world. Eating sushi is about varying aspects of

Japan is an island country surrounded by seas that are abundant with a huge variety of fish.

Delicate red mullet sashimi provides subtle and complex tastes and textures (page 190).

appreciation, from being delighted by the eye, intrigued by the texture, or captured by the lingering taste of the fresh, energising nature of the sea.

Sushi makes a very distinct impression without any one aspect being dominant or obvious. It is an art form and is considered an extension of nature in Japan, where food is so fresh that it tastes of the food itself and not what has been done to it. Ingredients are introduced in varying degrees of rawness, nothing is overcooked; one feels close to food in its natural state.

Developing an understanding of the integrity of the raw ingredients requires patience and skill, and thus a sushi chef in Japan will toil away cleaning the display fridge or fish tank or floor for the first few years of his apprenticeship, before being allowed to enter behind the sushi counter.

In a traditional sushi bar in Japan, one is seated in front of the sushi master, where he will deftly slice and meld the sushi in front of you. With speed and precision that comes from many years of training, he produces a couple of neat oblong-shaped nigiri with all the grains of rice, it is said, facing in the same direction. In this traditional environment the reverence that Japan holds for its food is illustrated in the relationship between diner and sushi master, where a quality of mutual trust and appreciation between the two is struck. The sushi master is, after all, preparing raw fish, which in the hands of an inexperienced chef could have undesirable consequences.

Sushi wasn't always this uplifting, though, as originally it was nothing more than a means of preserving fish for the inclement winter months, when fishing was dangerous. Rice was packed around the fish fillets and left to ferment, then discarded before the aging fish flesh was eaten.

Gradually, over centuries, this style of sushi became oshi zushi or pressed sushi, where layers of fish and rice are pressed down. This style is still found today (see pages 265 and 266), but the more commonly known nigiri-style sushi today is from Tokyo, and was introduced in the early 1800s. There is no fermenting, no pressing into moulds, no waiting. Thus sushi became the world's first fast food.

sushi etiquette

To describe sushi as 'parcels of vinegared rice with various toppings of usually fish or shellfish' does little to reveal its cultural subtleties and complexities. But a trip to a traditional sushi bar gives away a lot more. You will enter a sushi bar through the noren curtain. In days gone by, a dirty one used to signify a popular sushi bar, as it was customary to wipe your hands on the curtain as you left!

Once inside, you will be greeted with a welcoming 'Irrashaimase' from the sushi chefs standing behind the immaculate white cypress sushi counter. The sushi counter is the place to sit to soak up the atmosphere and be treated to the day's selection of best fish. You will be offered a wet towel, or oshibori, and a cup of hot sencha green tea, which is called agari rather than ocha in a sushi bar. The sushi master will lean over and put down a small dish of gari ginger pickle to refresh your palate between each sushi. It is considered unseemly to eat this all at once as one might a salad or garnish. Now you are settled in, you are ready to order.

Some like to start with slices of sashimi; others might want to dive straight into the sushi. Generally, one starts with nigiri sushi (pages 56–91), and in Japan these make up most of the sushi dinner, before moving on to gunkan (pages 92–121), and lastly maki or temaki sushi (pages 122–87, 220–45).

In the West, we tend to reverse this, preferring the more flamboyant flavours of a futomaki to the reserved ones of a nigiri. In any event, start with subtle, delicate whitefish, such as bream or snapper, before moving on to fattier fish such as salmon and tuna, or 'shiny' fish as they are called in Japan, like mackerel and herring.

Cooked seafood such as prawns or octopus are eaten towards the end of the nigiri selection. You will probably finish your sushi dinner with rolled sushi, and the chef might ask you whether you'd like it cut into 6 or 8 maki pieces or as a temaki hand roll.

It is commonplace not to order in a sushi bar, rather relying on the chef to size you up, and determine a suitable sushi course for you. Omakase dining (leave it up to the chef) is a wonderful way to enjoy sushi, but be warned – it is invariably not the cheapest. Refresh your palate with the gari ginger in between each type of sushi, especially after an oily fish such as mackerel, so as to cleanse the palate for your next morsel.

Be aware when you order at a sushi counter that nigiri and gunkan are always served in pairs, whilst hosomaki and futomaki come as whole rolls of six or eight pieces. Try to eat each nigiri and gunkan in one whole mouthful, as biting them in bits is not elegant.

Fill your soy sauce bowl with only enough to cover the bottom of the bowl. It is not good etiquette to fill it to the brim. It is considered courteous to pour the soy sauce for your guest. If you are eating both sushi and sashimi, you should have two bowls, one for your sashimi where you might want to add a small dab of wasabi to the bowl and mix it into the soy sauce. Or you can dab a little wasabi directly on the sashimi slices and dip gently into the soy sauce. The other bowl is for your sushi because it is not a good practice to add wasabi to your soy. The chef will already have seasoned the sushi with wasabi. Be aware it may even be considered insulting to add more wasabi to your sushi master's creations!

Deftly pick up the sushi and place it fish- or topping-side down into the soy, lightly dipping it rather than soaking it. If you place it rice-side down, the rice ball will fall apart and any subtle flavour is lost.

It is perfectly acceptable to not use chopsticks to eat sushi. Indeed, the more high-class or traditional the sushi bar, the more likely you are to eat sushi with your hands. There is something poignant about being handed sushi directly from a chef's masterful hands; using chopsticks puts a distance between you and your sushi master and breaks the spell.

Chopsticks are essential to eat just about everything else though, so it is best to get to grips with them to eat the sashimi, the pickles and the miso soup or any accompanying hot dishes. The best advice I can give for chopsticks is to hold them gently; gripping them seems to make maneuvering virtually impossible. When you are not eating with them, place the pointed ends that hold the food onto the chopstick rest, or if one isn't given, then rest them on the soy bowl. Never lick or suck your chopsticks.

Never stand them vertically in a bowl of rice or transfer food from your chopsticks to another's; both of these actions are more appropriate in some religious rituals than at the dinner table. Never use your own chopsticks in a shared plate of food; either use the serving chopsticks or if there are none, turn your chopsticks around the other way to serve yourself.

Miso soup or suimono clear soup usually come towards the end of the sushi dinner, and signifies that the diner is replete. Miso soup is never drunk as an starter in Japan.

a plea for our oceans

I find this section the hardest to write. When I started on my sushi journey, I knew little about the plight of our oceans, but now that I am aware of the destruction our global fishing industry has wreaked on our seas, I feel a real sadness for our waters and the beautiful creatures that live in them.

We are hugely reliant on the health of our seas; they absorb carbon for us, create temperate weather patterns, present a myriad of medical solutions, and above all provide much of the world with its main source of protein and good nutrition. And yet, like so many other things in life, we turn a blind eye to the devastation we have inflicted on nature. No less than 80 percent of fish stocks are fished to the maximum allowable level or are overfished. That leaves only 20 percent doing okay. We have a duty to care for the next generation and, indeed, to preserve the few resources that we have left.

I firmly believe that we can find a solution to the problems of our seas with a little help from Japanese philosophy. There is as much good as there is bad in the world, as much yin as there is yang, but our complicity or inertia can lead to the bad overriding the good. Instead, we need to play an active role in our choices. There is nothing more grounding and compassionate than the choices we make about what we eat.

Our collective choices can change the whole way we take fish from the seas. Changing habits of a lifetime doesn't happen overnight, though, so accept that change in the world's fishing industries will take a while. These days it is not hard to go online and find wonderful words of wisdom from Slow Food, Monterey Bay Aquarium, Greenpeace and the Marine Stewardship Council to name but a few. I urge you to get to know how your fish was caught; if we catch plentiful fish unsustainably, then they won't be sustainable for long.

The last word goes to Carlo Petrini, founder of the groundbreaking organisation Slow Food, and to whom I am most grateful for inspiring change in me: anyone who thinks of themselves as a food lover but does not have any environmental awareness is naïve – whereas an ecologist who does not enjoy the pleasures of food certainly has a sadder life.

japanese knives

It is said that the sushi master's knife is as precious to him as the sword is to a samurai. The yanagiba, long and narrow and pointed at the end, are often described as sashimi knives. Sushi chefs never share their yanagiba, and this is because it becomes an extension of their arm, finely tuned to be able to expertly slice and cut to the rhythm of their art.

A sushi chef will keep his yanagiba knife exceptionally sharp so as to maximise the flavour, texture and appearance of the fish. It is up to you which grade of knife you wish to use, but bear in mind that whilst the very expensive stainless steel knife keeps its sharpness well, it doesn't take well to the sharpening stone.

A sushi chef regularly sharpens his knife on sharpening stones (never a steel knife sharpener or an electric one) that vary in coarseness depending on the age and quality of the knife. When not in use, the knives should be wrapped in a clean, dry cloth.

If they are not to be used for a while, it is best to rub a little vegetable oil over the blade to prevent rusting. Japanese yanagiba knives differ from Western knives in that they are flat on one side. This enables the knife to slice through the fish flesh without causing the flesh to fray, leaving the flesh looking translucent and iridescent. True to so many things in Japan, the simplicity belies the complexity and the many other benefits of good cutting techniques.

The texture is one such very important feature. Westerners who say they don't like sushi or sashimi, never say that it doesn't taste good. Rather, it is the texture they cannot stand – the very feel of the food. The Japanese appreciate texture almost as much as they appreciate taste, so the contrast of warm, pliable grains of rice under a slice of cool, resilient fish exemplifies the unwritten rule of opposites being complementary. Last, the knives, like so many other elements in the making of sushi, play a key role in reducing the buildup of bacteria on the fish flesh. A well-kept knife produces cleaner, safer sushi as it reduces the surface area exposed to oxidisation.

Sake is the traditional Japanese rice wine that can be enjoyed, warm or cold, with sushi.

choosing and filleting fish

Look out for these signs when choosing your fish: the gills should be bright red, the eyes translucent and bright, the skin firm so that when you press a finger on the flesh it doesn't leave an indentation. It should be slimy to the touch, and it should smell of the sweetness of the sea and not at all fishy. If it does smell fishy, the fish's own enzymes have started to work on breaking down its flesh, and it is a sign that the fish is probably not palatable for eating raw. Don't forget to wash your hands before filleting fish to reduce the chance of a bacterial buildup.

sanmai oroshi 3-piece filleting round fish
Filleting in Japan is named after the number of pieces a fish is to be cut into, so, for example, quite simply, a bass is sanmai oroshi, or filleting into three.

Remove the scales with a sharp knife or scaler. You might find it handy to place the fish in a large plastic bag whilst you are doing this so as to not get fish scales scattered around your kitchen. Cut along under the gills where the head joins the body and remove the head. Cut open the stomach and remove the entrails, then clean out the dark red blood that is around the backbone area with a brush.

Wash the fish thoroughly. Place the fish on the chopping board and insert the knife into the back as far as the backbone and cut along the length of the fish from the head to the tail. Then turn the fish and insert the knife in the same fashion on the stomach side and remove the upper fillet. Do the same on the other side, first cutting in toward the backbone, then removing the second fillet from the stomach cut. The fish will now be in three pieces: two fillets and a backbone.

Remove the stomach bones from the two fillets by holding your knife horizontally and slicing them out of the fillets. Now cut each fillet into two along the line of the missing backbone. Last, cut off the parts with the tiny bones next to the cut you have just made. To remove the skin, place the fillets skin-side facing down on your board, gently insert the knife at the tail end between the skin and the flesh, and raise the blade slightly. Holding the tail end firmly in place with your left hand, run the blade along the bottom of the fish, cutting away the skin as thinly as possible.

As a general observation, always try to fillet whilst moving the knife in one long, sweeping motion, rather than hacking away. A cleanly cut fish improves the appearance of the sashimi, it enhances the texture on the palate, and importantly, it reduces the oxidisation of a jagged-edged flesh, which in turn prevents the flesh from deteriorating and the buildup of bacteria, very important considerations when eating fish raw.

squid & cuttlefish

You must make sure to use freshly caught squid as it will be eaten raw. It is best to use frozen squid if your fishmonger can't guarantee the freshness of the whole squid. If you are using a whole squid, place it on a chopping board. Holding the head in one hand, grasp the tentacles at their base and gently straighten them out with the other hand. Reach inside the body cavity and remove the translucent quill. Throw away the guts, trying not to pierce the ink sac, which can be retained if you'd like to use it.

Insert a knife into the body and carefully slit it down one side. Put a finger under the fin to separate it, and then pull off the fin and remove the thin membrane. Trim to remove the 'wings' that can be seen attached to the body. Cut away the tentacles just in front of the eyes and squeeze out the small beak. Rinse and pat dry. For cuttlefish, follow the same steps as for squid, but cut the head on the cuttle side, open and remove the guts. The ink sac is attached to the other side.

gomai oroshi – 5-piece filleting for flat fish

This filleting technique is used mostly on large flat fish and, if you are less confident, on smaller flat fish, too, because it is easier to split the fillets than try to remove them in one piece. There are no scales to remove on a flat fish. Now follow the steps for 3-piece filleting, cutting the boneless side of the fillet into two, creating four boneless fillets, with the fifth piece being the central skeleton.

To do this, place the fish belly down on the cutting board, and cut along the curve of the outer fins on both sides, then cut through the centre from tail to head. Pull the fillets off, starting at the centre of the head end, the firmest part, and pull the fish away from the bone. Do the same on the other side. Turn the fish over and repeat on the belly side.

Cutting at an angle, remove the stomach lining and pull out any small bones with tweezers. Skin the fillets the same way as described in 3-piece filleting.

preparing large fish for neta slices

Large fish such as tuna and hamachi yellowtail, and often salmon, are characterised by a fattier, more tender texture, and so are somewhat unsatisfying if cut into thin slices. Each slice should be cut into pieces 7.5–10-cm (3–4-in) long and 2.5 cm (1-in) wide. Each slice should weigh around 25 g (¾ oz). Cut at right angles to the sinews; if the fish is cut in parallel slices, some pieces may turn out white and hard.

The best tuna is often found for sale in Japan – Marinated Tuna Nigiri (page 58).

nigiri sushi technique

Whilst fish plays the starring role in sushi, it would be nothing without the supporting role of the rice. Indeed, the rice makes all the difference to the texture and enjoyment of the small morsel of fish on the palate. It is important that the rice is evenly flavoured and textured, and that the warmth of the rice ball complements the coolness of the fish. There is little worse than cold, compact rice on your sushi.

To make a perfect nigiri, try first to relax! Add about 2 tablespoons of vinegar to a small bowl of water. Wet your fingers and the palm of your left hand in it to help prevent the rice from sticking to your fingers and also to help sanitise them.

Place the neta (the generic term for any topping on a nigiri sushi) slice in your left hand. Lightly grip the end of the slice between your index finger and thumb, letting the slice rest lightly on the middle joints of your fingers. Now take a small ball of shari rice weighing about 15 g (½ oz) in your right hand and gently mould it to form the classic nigiri shape. Whilst cupping the shari rice loosely in the palm of your right hand, take some wasabi with the index finger of the right hand and smear it gently on the centre of the neta slice.

Place the shari rice ball on top of the neta slice. Gently curve the palm of your left hand, press firmly with the thumb of the same hand in the middle of the ball of rice to make an indentation. This ensures that the outside of the nigiri is firm whilst the inside remains sufficiently soft.

Roll the sushi down your left hand so it rests across the fingers of the left hand with the neta slice facing upwards. Press the end of the shari rice with your left thumb, then rotate 180 degrees to press gently on the other end.

Extend your right index finger and middle finger over the top of the neta slice, but without pressing down with this hand, shape the sushi using the left hand, pressing upwards. Pin both sides of the sushi between your right middle finger and thumb to shape, then rotate the sushi 180 degrees.

The finished nigiri shape should be even and, if you've managed to handle the shari and neta as little as possible, the nigiri should look as though it were about to swim off!

Smoked fish is a non-traditional but delicious addition to nigiri – Tea-Smoked Salmon Nigiri (page 64).

maki rolling technique: futomaki

In this method of rolling, one must be extremely careful to prevent the rice from bursting out of the nori and the fillings being crushed. Place a bowl of vinegared water on one side of your board. Place the nori, shiny-side down, on top of a maki rolling mat, with the longer edge nearest yourself. Lay clingfilm on your mat if you like.

Dip your fingers in the vinegared water and spread about 200 g (7 oz) of shari rice evenly over the nori, making sure you leave a 2-cm (3/4-in) gap of bare nori at the top (far side). Smear a dab of wasabi in the middle across the width of the roll. The amount would be to your taste. It's up to you now how you choose the fillings; always bear in mind the appearance and colour balance of the finished maki.

Now for the tricky part! Press lightly on the middle of the roll with your index and middle finger and pick up the side of the maki mat closest to you with your thumbs.

In one fluid motion, roll the maki mat forwards, enclosing the fillings but leaving the bare nori strip. Using your fingertips, bring the mat down to meet the bare strip of nori, to make sure the roll is sealed properly. Press on the sides of the mat to shape into a gentle square, then roll over 90 degrees and press again to shape.

Remove the mat, place it over the roll, and press down once more to shape the edges.

Cut into 6 or 8 pieces, using a sharp, clean knife dipped into a little water, pushing the pieces away from you as you cut.

maki rolling technique: uramaki

These are like futomaki rolls but are rolled in reverse so that the nori is on the inside and the outer layer is open to any number of different ingredients. It is a highly decorative way of making sushi and appeals to Westerners.

Place a bowl of vinegared water at one side. Cover the bamboo maki mat with clingfilm on both sides. Lay the sheet of nori on the plastic-covered mat with the long side facing you. Spread 200 g (7 oz) of shari rice evenly over the nori, covering it right up to the edges. Spread evenly on top of the rice whatever ingredient you choose to use on the outside of your roll. Fish roes such as tobiko are popular choices, and you can also use micro greens such as shiso cress or mustard and cress.

Deftly pick up the nori at the corners and flip it over so that the nori is now face up. Arrange the fillings along the centre of the nori. With your hands held over the base of the mat and pressing the mat down over the ingredients with your fingers as you go, roll the mat over the ingredients, leaving a 2.5-cm (1-in) piece of nori visible at the top.

Press gently to mould the roll together. Lift up the mat, roll back a little, then roll forwards to join the nori edges. Use gentle pressure to firm and mould the roll in the shape you like – square, oval or round. Unfurl the mat and, if desired, evenly spread a topping around the roll's outer side.

Using a sharp knife, cut into 8 pieces by cutting the roll in half, then each half in halves again. Then cut the 4 quarters one more time to make 8 even pieces. Alternatively, you can cut the roll into 6 pieces. Cut gently so as to maintain your chosen shape.

basic recipes

Soy sauce, miso, mirin, rice vinegar and dashi are

the main components of Japanese cuisine.

Familiarise yourself with these elegantly simple

components in their most widely used contexts, and

you will become confident enough to experiment.

tsuma – sashimi decoration

see variations page 46

Sashimi, raw fish served without rice, is never served solo. An unadorned slice of raw fish on a plate with nothing else is like eating bread without butter. Shredded vegetables such as daikon white radish and seaweeds are typically placed under, to the side of or sometimes as a garnish on top of the sashimi. The generic name for these garnishes is tsuma. Their purpose is not merely decorative, as they help cover up the smell of raw fish and provide some help with sterilising, whilst others aid digestion. They also add to the colour, texture and scent of a dish. Once again, we see the harmony of beauty to the eye being beneficial to the body, and in adding vegetables to fish, the balance of nature.

1 tsp of dried wakame seaweed
35-cm (14-in) long piece of daikon white radish

Soak the seaweed in a little water for a few minutes. Drain and squeeze out the water. With a 15-cm (6-in) long sharp knife, hold the daikon firmly against the knife and rotate the daikon gradually to produce one long uniform strip.

Fold the strip into thirds, and cut into fine shreds. Plunge into ice water for at least 15 minutes. Drain the daikon and mix with the wakame. Make a bed of wakame and daikon tsuma and arrange your sashimi slices on top.

Serves 2

shari sushi rice

see variations page 47

Choosing a good rice is important in sushi; it must, once cooked, have optimal absorbency qualities to ensure that the flavour of each rice grain is even and has a consistently soft and sticky texture. Use short grain japonica white rice, which can be found in all Japanese supermarkets and health food shops, or arborio, Italian risotto rice.

200 g (7 oz) short grain japonica rice
500 ml (17 fl. oz) water
100 ml (2½ fl. oz) rice vinegar

30 g (1 oz) sugar
1 tsp salt

Place the rice in a bowl and cover with cold water. Stir the water and the rice to allow the impurities and outer bran layers to be washed away. Gently rub the rice with the base of your palms to strip the rice of its outer layers. Discard the milky water. Repeat this process a number of times until the water runs clear. Put the draining rice into a sieve to stand for about 30 minutes. Put the rice and water into a rice cooker and cook for 10–15 minutes. Alternatively, place the rice and water in a heavy-bottomed saucepan, and cover tightly with a lid. Bring to a boil on medium heat and boil for 2–3 minutes. Reduce the heat to its lowest setting and simmer for a further 10–12 minutes. Resist the temptation to lift the lid!

Once cooked, leave in the rice cooker or remove the saucepan from the heat, and leave to stand without lifting the lid for an additional 15–20 minutes. Thoroughly mix the vinegar, sugar and salt together in a saucepan and heat gently over a low flame until the sugar and salt are dissolved. Remove from the heat and allow to cool. Pour water into the wooden rice tub and leave to absorb. Tip out the water and wipe with a dry dishcloth. Place the cooked rice in the pre-soaked wooden rice tub or in a flat-bottomed, non-metallic bowl if you don't

have a rice tub. Spread the rice over the flat bottom of the tub with a spatula. Slowly add the vinegar mixture by pouring it onto the spatula and allowing it to flow onto the rice. Quickly mix the rice and vinegar together with the spatula, using a slicing action to coat the grains of rice evenly and to separate them.

Fan the shari rice mixture to cool the surface temperature to about skin temperature. Transfer the cooled shari rice into a container and cover with a damp cloth. Keeping the temperature of the shari rice slightly warm is crucial; when cooled, the starch in the rice looses its absorbency and the texture in the mouth will be uneven and hard. Too hot, on the other hand, will impair the freshness of the topping on the rice, so keeping shari rice at around body temperature is ideal.

Serves 4

miso soup

see variations page 48

Miso is the very soul of Japan. Made with traditional methods, it is rich in vitamins and high in protein and also has an amazing ability to rid the body of toxins. If you're feeling a little run down in the morning, miso soup is a great pick-me-up!

1 block of silken tofu
30 g (1 oz) wakame seaweed
1 l (40 fl. oz) dashi stock (page 44)

60 g (2 oz) of mugi miso paste (per bowl)
2 chopped spring onions

Strain the tofu and cut the tofu block into 1-cm (⅓-in) cubes. Rehydrate the wakame seaweed in a bowl with cold water for about 5 minutes or until soft. (Read the packet, as sometimes the wakame doesn't need rehydrating.) Squeeze the water out and chop into 2-cm (¾-in) lengths.

Place the dashi in a saucepan and bring to the boil. Stir a little of the dashi water into the miso paste to thin it before adding it to the dashi water. Lower the heat and stir as the soup simmers gently. Place the tofu cubes and wakame in miso bowls, ladle out the miso soup and garnish with chopped spring onion.

Serves 2

gari pickled ginger

see variations page 49

Historically, when much of the available arable land was given up to rice production, pickles were used as a means of staying healthy and were pretty much the only vegetable consumed throughout the winter months when fresh vegetables became scarce. Another reason for their popularity is their infinite versatility. They are made with many different types of vegetables; regional variations are great sources of local pride. Pickles have come to signify the end of a meal in Japan. Their appearance is so anticipated that even after a full meal the Japanese will feel that something is missing until the tsukemono arrive. Pickled ginger, however, holds a slightly different place in the world of pickles. Gari, pickled sushi ginger, as it is known exclusively in sushi restaurants, is made to be eaten sparingly between the different sushi rather than at the end of a sushi meal.

200 g (7 oz) fresh, young ginger, peeled and
    sliced into long, thin diagonals
4 tsp sea salt

200 ml (6 fl. oz) rice vinegar
4 tsp sugar
20 g (¾ oz) red shiso leaf

Place the slices of ginger in a bowl, sprinkle on the salt and leave for about an hour. Transfer the ginger slices into a sterilised jar. In a separate container, stir together the rice vinegar and sugar until the sugar has dissolved.

Pour the rice vinegar liquid over the ginger pieces in the jar. Add the red shiso leaves, put the lid on the jar and store in the refrigerator at least overnight, and up to a week. It is the addition of the red shiso leaf that gives gari its pale pink colour.

Serves 4

yuzu mayonnaise

see variations page 50

The use of mayonnaise in sushi started in California and was later introduced into Japan. I'm not a big fan of smothering my sushi in any form of mayonnaise, mostly because it, in my opinion, serves only to mask the subtle flavours of the ingredients and detracts from the texture. I would thus recommend using the following recipes as dipping sauces (alternatives to soy sauce) rather than adding it to maki rolls, but your own palate will let you know how you feel about using it.

2 yolks from large eggs
1 tsp mustard powder
1 clove of crushed garlic
250 ml (9 fl. oz) peanut oil

1 tsp rice vinegar
1 tsp light soy sauce
1/2 tsp yuzu zest

Make sure all the ingredients are at room temperature. Place the egg yolks in a bowl and add the mustard powder and garlic. Mix well together. With an electric beater in one hand (or a wire whisk) and a jug of peanut oil in the other hand, start to add the oil to the egg yolk mixture drop by drop. At the beginning, be sure that each drop of oil is whisked in before adding the next drop to prevent curdling.

After a while the mixture will start to thicken. When about half the oil is mixed in, add the rice vinegar. Once all the oil is thoroughly whisked in, add the soy sauce and yuzu zest and mix well. Set aside and chill.

Makes about 350 ml (12 fl. oz)

teriyaki sauce

see variations page 51

Beware of just how much sugar or sweetener you are using in your Japanese dishes and where possible use an alternative such as honey or apple juice, or buy good brands of mirin (outside of Japan I have only come across the Clearspring brand, which is truly heavenly).

roasted chicken thigh bones
roasted leek tops
300 ml (10 fl. oz) dark soy sauce

125 ml (4 fl. oz) sake
125 ml (4 fl. oz) hon-mirin
2 tbsp honey

You can either grill or roast the chicken bones and leeks. Add the roasted chicken bones and leek tops to a saucepan then combine all the liquid ingredients except the honey in the pan. Bring it to the boil and gently simmer for 20 minutes until the sauce has thickened. Add the honey and stir for a further 5 minutes.

It is worth noting that most Japanese recipes I have looked at recommend equal portions of mirin to soy and one-third volume of sugar, so if the above recipe isn't what you are looking for, feel free to play around with the ratios or add sugar!

Makes about 600 ml (20 fl. oz)

ponzu

see variations page 52

Ponzu is a tangy citrus-flavoured soy sauce, and its simple clean flavour complements most whitefish, as well as 'shiny' ones such as horse mackerel. It can also be used in more modern dishes and is great in salad dressings.

1 43-cm (17-in) square piece of konbu kelp
8 tbsp soy sauce
8 tbsp rice vinegar
2 tbsp lemon juice

Combine all the ingredients and leave overnight in a refrigerator. Remove the konbu before using the ponzu.

Makes about 250 ml (9 fl. oz)

saikyo miso

see variations page 53

This incredibly simple topping is best known for doing amazing things to aubergine!

120 ml (4 fl. oz) sake
120 ml (4 fl. oz) mirin

200 g (7 oz) white miso paste
3 tbsp sugar

Bring the sake and mirin to the boil in a saucepan over a high heat and boil for a few seconds to cook off the alcohol.

Turn down the heat and add the miso paste, mixing with a wooden spoon. When the miso has dissolved, turn up the heat again and add the sugar, stirring constantly to prevent the sauce from sticking. Remove from the heat once the sugar has dissolved.

Makes about 750 ml (24 fl. oz)

ceviche sauce

see variations page 54

The following recipes are inspired by the flavours of South America. Ceviche cooking has been championed in Japanese restaurants by Nobuyuki Matsuhisa at his restaurant, Nobu. The ceviche sauce is best paired with chopped, leftover pieces of shellfish or whitefish. The citrus and oil semi-poach the raw flesh. It is good Zen not to waste, and this recipe helps achieve that.

1 red onion	2 tbsp dashi
3 cloves garlic	1 tbsp soy sauce
1 fresh jalapeño	2 tsp lime juice
1 red chilli with seeds	3 tbsp olive oil
1 shiso leaf	150 ml (5 fl. oz) shiso juice
1 spring onion stem	sprinkle of sesame seeds

Roughly chop the onion, garlic, jalapeño, chilli, shiso leaf and spring onion. Mix the dashi, soy, lime juice, olive oil and shiso juice. Blend all the sauce ingredients together.

Sprinkle in the sesame seeds.

Makes about 375 ml (12 fl. oz)

dashi stock

see variations page 55

Dashi is the basic stock in Japan. Unlike its Western counterparts, dashi is quick and easy to make, relying, as so much of Japan's food does, on the integrity, quality and skill that has gone into producing its ingredients.

30 g (1 oz) or 1 piece of dried kelp konbu about 10 cm (4-in) long

1.75 l (60 fl. oz) water
1 tbsp katsuo dried bonito flakes

Do not wipe the white glutamate deposits from the surface of the konbu – this is precisely the umami flavour that you seeking to extract. Place the konbu in a saucepan with the water and bring to the boil.

Simmer for 15–20 minutes until the liquid is reduced. Remove the konbu and bring to the boil again. Add 4 tablespoons of cold water and the katsuo flakes. Allow to infuse for 5 minutes. Sieve the liquid to remove the katsuo and set aside the clear dashi.

Makes about 1.5 l (50 fl. oz)

variations

tsuma – sashimi decoration

see base recipe page 27

shiso leaf

Shiso leaf is a quintessentially Japanese sushi ingredient. Its beautiful light green or red leaves impart colour and vibrancy to a plate of sashimi, and it has a fragrance and flavour quite unlike any other herb. Shiso has powerful antibacterial properties, which is always a consideration when dealing with raw ingredients that can easily deteriorate. It contains a lot of vitamins and minerals that are a good boost to the immune system, are particularly good in treating allergies and have a beneficial effect on the skin.

mixed seaweed tsuma

There are virtually no calories in seaweed, and it contains high amounts of vitamins A, B, C and E in addition to minerals, in particular, iodine, as well as calcium, magnesium and iron. Moreover, it is high in omega-3. Combining different coloured seaweeds makes a really attractive tsuma or even a salad.

hijiki seaweed & daikon tsuma

Hijiki is brown seaweed and looks like stems of tea on a plate. Its lustrous black contrasts well with the gleaming white of the radish. It is usually available in dried form and, depending on the brand, generally needs simmering for about 30 minutes before using in the tsuma.

cucumber & daikon tsuma

Peel a length of cucumber the same way as the daikon radish and mix together.

variations

shari sushi rice

see base recipe page 28

genmai brown rice
Replace the uncooked rice with genmai short-grain brown rice. The water will be less milky in the washing process. Follow the same cooking and mixing steps but double the amount of water used in the rice cooking process.

gomoku rice or 5-grain rice
Gomoku rice translates as 'five grain', or 'five things', but in fact you can choose any number of different grains to suit your taste. Grains to chose from might include millet, adzuki bean, black rice, soybean, red rice, black sesame and white sesame. Follow the same cooking steps but double the amount of water.

low-sugar shari rice
Generally, the ratio of vinegar to rice is about 15 percent, but you can adjust the salt and sugar as you like. You'll find the right balance as you become more practiced, but salt amounts typically range from a small pinch to about ¾ teaspoon per 7 tablespoons of uncooked rice, and sugar from ¾ tablespoon to as much as 4 teaspoons.

sake & konbu shari rice
If you are eager to retain a good flavour but also reduce the amount of sugar or salt, then add a 7.5-cm (3-in) strip of konbu dried kelp to the rice pot before cooking, or add a little sake rice wine to the mixture. Both are very traditional practices in Japan.

variations

miso soup

see base recipe page 30

red miso, burdock & carrot
Prepare the basic recipe, replacing mugi miso with red miso paste. Blanch a few julienned pieces of burdock and carrot, and add a splash of sesame oil.

red miso, shiitake mushroom & nira garlic shoots
Prepare the basic recipe, replacing mugi miso with red miso paste. Add a few blanched pieces of shiitake mushroom and nira garlic shoots.

saikyo miso & snapper
Prepare the basic recipe, replacing mugi miso with saikyo miso. Pour a little boiling water over 2.5-cm (1-in) lengths of a whitefish fillet. Chop a few trefoil mitsuba leaves or chives and add them and a few spinach leaves.

saikyo miso & lotus root
Prepare the basic recipe, replacing mugi miso with saikyo miso. Cut a lotus root into 1.25-cm (½-in) thick slices, chop these into quarters and lightly blanche them. Add two pieces of lotus root to each bowl of miso soup.

gochujang miso stew
Prepare the basic recipe. Stir in a teaspoon of gochujang Korean chilli paste. For each bowl of miso, add a few blanched, 2-cm (¾-in) chunks Chinese cabbage, a small bunch enoki mushrooms, a couple of 2-cm (¾-in) lengths nira garlic chives, and 4 pieces diced tofu.

gari pickled ginger

see base recipe page 32

salted cucumber pickles
Prepare the basic recipe, replacing ginger with small Japanese cucumbers. Slice the cucumbers and cover with salt. Leave under a heavy weight at least overnight.

vinegared & wasabi cucumber pickles
Prepare the basic recipe, replacing ginger with cubed cucumber. Smear with a little wasabi.

daikon white radish in sake pickles
Prepare the basic recipe, replacing ginger with sliced white radish and replacing half the rice vinegar with sake rice wine.

aubergine pickles
Prepare the basic recipe, replacing ginger with small Japanese aubergines.

kanpyo calabash gourd pickles
Prepare the basic recipe, replacing ginger with calabash. The pieces of gourd often come in dried form, so they first need to be rehydrated overnight in water. Replace rice vinegar with sake rice wine and salt. Add a few sesame seeds.

chinese cabbage & chilli pickles
Prepare the basic recipe, replacing ginger with slices of salted Chinese cabbage and chopped chilli.

variations

yuzu mayonnaise

see base recipe page 34

wasabi mayonnaise
Prepare the basic recipe, replacing yuzu zest with freshly grated wasabi root. Omit the mustard powder.

gochujang Korean chilli mayonnaise
Prepare the basic recipe, omitting the mustard powder and replacing yuzu zest with up to 1 tablespoon of gochujang (Korean chilli paste).

smoked paprika mayonnaise
Prepare the basic recipe, omitting the mustard powder and rice vinegar, and replacing yuzu zest with ¼ teaspoon smoked paprika, juice of 1 lemon and freshly ground black pepper.

sweet chilli mayonnaise
Prepare the basic recipe, omitting the mustard powder. Replace yuzu zest with up to 1 tablespoon of Thai sweet chilli sauce.

tonkatsu mayonnaise
Prepare the basic recipe, omitting the mustard powder and replacing yuzu zest with up to 1 tablespoon of tonkatsu sauce, or Worcestershire sauce.

variations

teriyaki sauce

see base recipe page 36

teriyaki with gochujang (korean chilli) sauce
Prepare the basic recipe, adding 3 tablespoons of gochujang with the honey.

thickened teriyaki sauce
Prepare the basic recipe, adding a teaspoon of kuzu starch to the sauce when simmering.

chilli & sesame teriyaki sauce
Prepare the basic recipe, adding a dessertspoon of sesame oil and 1 finely chopped red chilli.

ginger teriyaki sauce
Prepare the basic recipe, adding a teaspoon of oroshi grated ginger.

variations

ponzu

see base recipe page 39

wafu salad dressing
Prepare the basic recipe, adding 6 tablespoons peanut oil, 1 tablespoon mirin, 1 tablespoon toasted sesame oil and a little Japanese mustard.

tamari wafu dressing
Prepare the basic recipe, replacing the soy sauce with tamari for a wheat-free ponzu and add to the above recipe.

ponzu butter
Heat a tablespoon of butter in a saucepan. Once melted, add 2 tablespoons of ponzu and combine together over a low heat. This is a nice sauce to spoon over some of the sushi recipes that use meat or cooked shellfish.

tofu sesame salad dressing
Combine half a block of tofu with 1 tablespoon toasted sesame oil, 2 tablespoons sunflower oil, 3 tablespoons ponzu, a little white miso paste and minced garlic.

yuzu vinaigrette
Combine 2 teaspoons Dijon mustard, 75 ml (2$\frac{1}{2}$ fl. oz) sesame oil, 125 ml (4 fl. oz) olive oil, 120 ml (4 fl. oz) rice vinegar, 250 ml (8 fl. oz) light soy sauce, 250 ml (8 fl. oz) yuzu juice (or 125 ml (4 fl. oz) lime juice if you can't find yuzu juice), 125 ml (4 fl. oz) dashi, 4 tablespoons sugar or 4 tablespoons concentrated apple juice and $\frac{1}{2}$ medium onion finely chopped.

variations

saikyo miso

see base recipe page 40

sesame dressing
Thoroughly mix together 1 tablespoon goma tare tahini paste, $\frac{1}{2}$ tablespoon sesame oil,
1 tablespoon soy sauce, $\frac{1}{4}$ teaspoon grated garlic, $\frac{1}{4}$ teaspoon grated ginger, $\frac{3}{4}$ tablespoon
rice vinegar, $\frac{1}{2}$ tablespoon runny honey, a squeeze of lemon juice and up to 2 tablespoon
dashi stock. Add dashi stock to adjust the viscosity of the sauce.

creamy spicy white miso dip
Combine equal portions of saikyo miso with wasabi mayonnaise.

variations

ceviche sauce

see base recipe page 43

jalapeño salsa

Combine 2 finely chopped jalapeños, 7 tablespoons finely chopped onions, 30 g (1 oz) chopped coriander, 30 g (1 oz) chopped flat-leaf parsley, 1 tablespoon soy sauce, ½ tablespoon rice vinegar, ¼ teaspoon chilli oil and 1 tablespoon olive oil. Serve immediately.

korean chilli sauce

Combine 3 tablespoons chilli pepper paste (gochujang), 3 tablespoons vinegar, ½ tablespoon sugar, 1 tablespoon apple juice, 1 tablespoon sesame seeds, 1 tablespoon chopped spring onion and ½ bowl sesame oil.

apple–mustard sauce

Grate half an apple, a 1½-in length of ginger and half a small onion (all oroshi style). Combine 125 ml (4 oz) rice vinegar, 2½ tablespoons grapeseed oil, 2½ tablespoons toasted sesame oil, 2 tablespoons sake and 4 teaspoons soy. Mix this liquid together with the oroshi ingredients, and then add a teaspoon of shichimi pepper, a teaspoon of toasted sesame seeds and a heaped tablespoon of coarse-grain mustard.

variations

dashi stock

see base recipe page 44

vegetarian dashi stock
Soak two pieces of 15-cm (6-in) long konbu and three dried shiitake mushrooms in about
1.5 l (48 oz) water for at least half an hour. Then bring the liquid to the boil and simmer
gently for 15 minutes. Strain off the konbu and shiitake and set aside the vegetarian dashi
to cool.

tempura dipping sauce
In a saucepan, combine 250 ml (8 oz) dashi stock, 60 ml (2 oz) hon-mirin, and 60 ml (2 oz)
soy sauce and mix well. Bring to the boil over a medium heat for 2 minutes.

nigiri sushi

The nigiri form of sushi is the classic style formed in Edo (old Tokyo) in the 1820s with the advent of the wider use of rice vinegar and sugar. It is hailed as being the first example of the type of sushi that is familiar to us today and in Japan is by far the most commonly found in a typical sushi dinner.

salmon nigiri

see variations page 79

Ironically, when I first visited Japan in the 1980s, it wasn't possible to obtain salmon, a freshwater fish, in its raw form. This changed with the huge increase of farmed salmon in the 1990s, and salmon is now one of Japan's top five fish for eating. If you are going to use wild salmon, it is advisable to choose a whole salmon of about 4 kg (9 lbs), and one before it has laid eggs, after which the flesh deteriorates significantly.

500 g (17 oz) fillet of salmon, skin on	wasabi
700 g (23 oz) shari rice (page 28)	soy sauce

Remove the skin from the fillet. Hold the knife at a 45 degree angle to the fish and cut diagonal slices so that each piece has a slight taper. Applying a quite firm pressure with your fingers to the fillet, slice through the remainder of the fillet to form even slices.

Use the technique described on pages 20–1 to shape the shari rice ball and make your salmon nigiri. The finished salmon nigiri shape should be even and, if you've managed to handle the shari and salmon as little as possible, the nigiri should look as though it were about to swim away!

Typically, one would serve two nigiri sushi at a time. With a bowl of soy sauce in place, gently dip the sushi, salmon side down, into the soy sauce and eat immediately.

Makes about 45 pieces

marinated tuna nigiri

see variations page 80

Before the introduction of flash-freezing at sea, the Japanese often used the following technique as a means of preserving fish. As tuna stocks dwindle, the quality of tuna becomes increasingly irregular, but this marinade will greatly improve any tuna recipe.

250 ml (8 fl. oz) soy sauce
125 ml (4 fl. oz) cup mirin
125 ml (4 fl. oz) sake
500 g (17 oz) tuna fillet
bowl of ice water

700 g (23 oz) shari rice
chopped spring onion
grated ginger
wasabi

Place the soy sauce, mirin, and sake in a saucepan and gently bring to the boil. Remove from the heat and allow to cool. Cut the fillet of tuna into 7.5-cm (3-in) long blocks. Place the blocks in a colander and cover with a clean cloth. Pour boiling water over the cloth-covered fish. When the surface of the fish has changed colour, turn it over and repeat on the other side. Remove the cloth and immediately place the tuna in a bowl of ice water. Pat dry when cooled. Place the tuna blocks in the soy marinade and allow to soak for 30–40 minutes. Using a slender-bladed yanagiba knife, hold the knife parallel to the fish, and cut slices from the block. Each slice should be around 6.25–7.5 cm (2½–3 in) long, 2.5 cm (1 in) wide, and 0.5 cm (¼ in) thick, and weigh about 15 g (½ oz) each.

Cut the fish at right angles to its sinews. Otherwise, whole slices of nigiri topping may be white in appearance and hard and chewy. Make each nigiri in the same way as described on pages 20–1. Top each nigiri with a sprinkling of chopped spring onion and grated ginger.

Makes about 20 pieces

mackerel nigiri

see variations page 81

Mackerel's richness in omega-3 oils makes it tasty and good for us. A vinegar marinade accentuates its natural flavours, and also eradicates the bacteria often found in oily fish.

2 mackerel fillets of about 200 g (6–7 oz) each
  (from large mackerel of preferably over
  1 kg/2 lbs)
4 tbsp of sea salt

250 ml (8 fl. oz) rice vinegar
400 g (12 oz) shari rice
chopped spring onion
grated ginger

Fillet the mackerel in the sanmai 3 part method (page 16). Place the mackerel fillet skin-side down in a bamboo colander covered with half of the salt. Sprinkle the remainder of the salt evenly on top of the mackerel fillets and place in the refrigerator for 45 minutes until the salt is dissolved. Then rinse the fish in cold water and pat dry. Place the fillets skin-side down in a clean flat-bottomed container and pour the rice vinegar over to cover the fillets entirely. Set aside to marinate for between 30 minutes and 1 hour, depending on the size of the fish. (The flesh should be faintly red inside; if totally white, it has been left too long). Remove the fillets from the vinegar and drain. Place on a chopping board and gently run your fingers across the flesh to find the bones. Remove the bones with a tweezer.

Cover with clingfilm or a damp cloth and store in the refrigerator until you are ready to make your nigiri. Slice the mackerel into about 3-mm (1/8-in) thick pieces, weighing about 20 g (1/2 oz) each. Make diagonal slashes in the skin to reveal the contrast between the shiny silver skin and the redder flesh inside. Make the mackerel nigiri with the technique shown on pages 20–1. Top with chopped spring onion and grated ginger.

Makes about 20 pieces

lobster tail & yuzu mayonnaise nigiri

see variations page 82

Crustaceans look wonderful on top of nigiri sushi, adding colour and texture to a sushi feast. They are one of the few ingredients in nigiri that are often cooked.

300 g (10 oz) lobster, boiled (just the tail
   is fine)
400 g (12 oz) shari rice (page 28)
nori sheet

120 g (4 oz) yuzu mayonnaise (page 34)
chopped spring onion

Have a large saucepan ready with enough water to cover the lobster and a bowl of ice water to hand. Live lobsters can be humanely killed beforehand by putting them in a plastic bag in the freezer for about two hours.

Scald the lobster in boiling water for 4 minutes, then plunge into the ice water. Remove the meat from the shell when cooled. Cut the tail into pieces about 7.5 cm (3 in) long each, and 2.5 cm (1 in) wide. Make each nigiri in the same way as described on pages 20–1.

Run a band of nori around the nigiri to secure the lobster chunk if it doesn't feel as though it will stay in place (not pictured). Top each nigiri lobster morsel with a teaspoon of yuzu mayonnaise and spring onion.

Makes about 20 pieces

tea-smoked salmon nigiri

see variations page 83

Smoked fish aren't traditionally used in sushi, but if you have doubts about the quality or freshness of your fish, then smoking it is a tasty and safe way to prepare it. Raw salmon, mackerel and some other fish present a significant risk of the parasite anisakis: only freezing these for at least 24 hours at temperatures beyond most home freezers' capability (below -31°C/-24°F) ensures safety. It's best to leave this to professionals.

3 tbsp hojicha green tea leaves
3 tbsp uncooked rice
5 tsp brown sugar
5 tsp sesame seeds
1 clove garlic, unpeeled

450 g (16 oz) salmon fillet
400 g (12 oz) shari rice (page 28)
120 g (4 oz) wasabi mayonnaise (page 50)
shiso cress or mustard and cress

Mix the hojicha, rice, sugar, sesame seeds and garlic together for the smoking mixture. Cover the base of a wok with aluminium foil and empty the smoking mixture onto it. Place the colander or steamer into a wok. Place the salmon into the steamer, cover and smoke for 8 minutes over a medium heat. If you don't have a steamer or colander, cover the mix with tin foil and lay the salmon on top.

Don't peek until the 8 minutes have gone by. It's best to take the wok outside before you lift the lid as there will be a lot of smoke. Take off the lid, and when the smoke has gone, you will be left with wonderful hot tea-smoked salmon. When cool enough to cut, slice into pieces, each about 7.5-cm (3-in) long, 2.5-cm (1-in) wide and 0.5-cm (¼-in) thick. Make each nigiri in the same way as described on pages 20–1. Top each nigiri with a teaspoon of wasabi mayonnaise and shiso cress or mustard and cress.

Makes about 20 pieces

foie gras & pomegranate nigiri

see variations page 84

Most unconventional, but decadent and delicious. Take your time to find foie gras reared without cruelty – I'm sure a happy goose will taste better, and you'll feel better. You can always try this with Japan's famed 'foie gras of the sea', monkfish liver (page 206).

250 g (8 oz) foie gras (goose liver)
potato flour, for coating
125 ml (4 fl. oz) rice vinegar
250 ml (8 fl. oz) soy sauce
125 ml (4 fl. oz) mirin

truffle oil
1 tbsp pomegranate seeds
400g (12 oz) shari rice (page 28)
nori strips
chopped leek

Heat a sharp knife under boiling water and cut the foie gras into 1.75-cm (³/₄-in) nigiri slices. Coat with potato flour. Preheat a non-stick frying pan over medium heat without using oil. Sear the foie gras on each side until golden brown with a crispy surface. It might be prudent to do it piece by piece, taking care not to break them. Drain on kitchen towels.

In the same frying pan, leave a little of the foie gras oil and add the rice vinegar, soy and mirin. Over a high heat, boil the sauce gently to reduce. Add a splash of truffle oil. When the sauce has reduced and thickened, add some pomegranate seeds.

Make the nigiri rice balls as described on pages 20–1 and put them on a chopping board. Carefully arrange the foie gras on top and secure with a strip of nori (not pictured). Top with chopped leek and a few more pomegranate seeds. Spoon the sauce over the nigiri when ready to eat.

Makes about 20 pieces

yubiki scalded red snapper nigiri

see variations page 85

Snappers and breams are generally referred to as tai in Japan, and cover as many as 200 different species. The common thread between them from a sushi perspective is their firm and even-textured flesh, with a relatively low fat content and simple yet distinctive flavour. They are held in great regard in Japan. Simple, salt-grilled tai is common at New Year and birthday celebrations.

300 g (10 oz) red snapper fillet
sea salt, for preparation and garnish
bowl of ice water

400 g (12 oz) shari rice (page 28)
zest of one lime

Snapper has a delicious fatty skin, but its toughness makes it difficult to eat. For this reason, a technique known as yubiki, where the skin is scalded, is commonly used. Only the skin is cooked, whilst the flesh underneath remains raw.

Place the fillet of snapper on a bamboo colander with the skin facing upwards and sprinkle with sea salt. Place a thin cloth over the fish and pour boiling water over it, working from the tail to the head (in the opposite direction of the line of the scales). Quickly immerse in a bowl of ice water.

When cool enough to cut, slice into pieces about 7.5 cm (3 in) long, 2.5 cm (1 in) wide, and 3 mm ($^1/_8$ in) thick. Make each nigiri the same way described on pages 20–1. Top with a sprinkle of lime zest and sea salt.

Makes about 20 pieces

aburi hamachi yellowtail

see variations page 86

Aburi, or seared sushi, was developed nearly a century ago in Japan. The act of applying fire directly and lightly, as a sear, is known to enhance the natural flavours of the fish.

300 g (10 oz) hamachi yellowtail fillet
400 g (12 oz) shari rice (page 28)

grated Parmesan cheese
chopped chives

Requires a blowtorch. Slice the yellowtail fillet into pieces about 7.5 cm (3 in) long, 2.5 cm (1 in) wide, and about 3 mm ($\frac{1}{8}$ in) thick. Make each nigiri the same way as described on pages 20–1.

Place the nigiri on a stainless steel tray and sprinkle them with the grated Parmesan cheese. Gently blowtorch the surface of the yellowtail until it becomes charcoaled on the outside. Top with chopped chives.

You will have noticed by now that the nigiri are always served in pairs, never as a single piece or in threes. It is thought that if one says 'one piece' in Japanese (hito kire), it sounds like the word used for murder, and the words for three pieces (mi kire) are like the words for suicide. Thus, two pieces of nigiri are both safe to request and, perhaps above all, just the right amount to savour.

Makes about 20 pieces

grilled shishito pepper nigiri

see variations page 87

Vegetarian sushi is quite limited in traditional Japanese sushi bars but has become increasingly popular in the West with the desire to rely less heavily on animal protein and go for low-calorie options. Certainly, a sushi lunch is low in calories, in spite of all the sugar and rice! A typical sushi lunch box meal contains fewer than 500 calories.

20 shishito, or Spanish pedron, peppers
250 ml (8 fl. oz) dashi (page 44)
1 tbsp light soy sauce
³/₄ tbsp mirin

1 tbsp sake
400 g (12 oz) shari rice (page 28)
120 ml (4 fl. oz) smoked paprika mayonnaise
(page 50)

This recipe starts with one of the classic forms of Japanese cooking, a nimono or simmered/poached dish. Trim the stems of the peppers. In a saucepan, add the dashi stock, soy sauce, mirin and sake, and bring gently to the boil. Add the peppers and simmer gently for about 2 minutes. This is your basic nimono dish. Remove the peppers from the saucepan and place under a grill for 1 minute, or until the skins of the peppers are lightly browned.

Make each nigiri in the same way as described in on pages 20–1. Top with a dot of smoked paprika mayonnaise.

Makes about 20 pieces

octopus nigiri

see variations page 88

Octopus and squid are often eaten raw in Japan, but can also be cooked to tenderise the flesh, which we will explore in this recipe.

1.5 kg (48 oz) whole octopus
1 tbsp sea salt
250 ml (8 fl. oz) dark soy sauce

125 ml (4 fl. oz) mirin
125 ml (4 fl. oz) sake
800 g (28 oz) shari rice (page 28)

Choose a large whole octopus (the smaller species are not suitable for sushi). A large frozen octopus will work well, too. Cut where the tentacles join the head and remove the beak with your fingers. Turn the head inside out and remove the innards. Rinse well under cold water and remove any sinewy bits. There are a number of ways to tenderise the octopus, none of which seem very conventional! Either pound the octopus flesh with half a raw daikon or, when boiling, add a tea bag. Fill a large saucepan with enough water to cover the octopus, add a tablespoon of sea salt, and bring to the boil. Tentacles first, place the octopus in the boiling water. Bring to the boil again, then lower the heat and simmer gently with the lid on for about 30 minutes. To keep the skin undamaged, make sure that the octopus isn't jiggling about. Take the saucepan off the heat and leave the octopus in the water to cool.

Bring the soy, mirin and sake gently to the boil. Lower the heat and simmer to reduce the liquid for about 15 minutes. Remove from the heat and leave to cool. Cut the octopus tentacles into nigiri-shaped slices and make the nigiri as described on pages 20–1. Wrap a piece of nori around the octopus. With a pastry brush, lightly brush the octopus with the soy mixture.

Makes about 40 pieces

scorched plaice nigiri

see variations page 89

Yuzu is a citrus fruit unique to Japan, with no foreign equivalent. The flesh is rarely used, but the zest and juice are valued as much for their aroma as for their flavour.

¹/₄ medium white daikon (radish)
1 tsp yuzukosho

130 g (10 oz) plaice (flatfish) fillet
400 g (12 oz) shari rice (page 28)

Using a flat grater, grate the white radish until it becomes almost a paste. Add a heaping teaspoon of yuzukosho and mix together. You can use any flatfish in this dish; choose one that is local and sustainably caught in your area. Even though the fish is scorched, a fresher fish will not only taste better but its flesh will retain a better texture. Fillet as you would for a nigiri. Fillet the plaice using the gomoi oroshi technique described on page 18. Slice into nigiri neta (pieces) of about 15 g (¹/₂ oz) each. Score the top of each neta with a sharp knife to make even lines across the top. This adds to both the appearance and texture of the sushi. Make the nigiri as described on pages 20–21.

When you have your nigiri ready, place two skewers under the grill or on top of a barbecue until scorching hot. Carefully pick up the hot skewers and with them scorch the top of each nigiri to produce charcoaled lines running across the flesh. Top with the grated radish mixture.

Makes about 20 pieces

tataki beef & caviar nigiri

see variations page 90

'Tataki' means to pound, and refers to the finely minced ingredients, often ginger or garlic, that are served with meat or fish for added flavour. These ingredients are usually served alongside, or used to marinate, seared meat or fish.

1 tbsp oroshi ginger
1 tbsp oroshi garlic
1 leek
450 g (14 oz) beef fillet, around 3.75-cm
    (1½-in) thick

vegetable oil, for frying
400 g (12 oz) shari rice (page 28)
skewers, for grilling
15g (1/2 oz) caviar

Using a flat grater, grate the ginger then garlic until they become almost a paste. Finely slice a 5-cm (2-in) length of leek. Trim the beef fillet. Heat a little vegetable oil in a small pan and quickly pan fry each side of the fillet for around 1 minute on each side, so as to brown the outside but leave the inside pink.

Slice the fillet into 7.5-cm (3-in) long, 3.75-cm (1½-in) wide, very thin slices. Make the nigiri as described on pages 20–1. Once you have your nigiri, take two skewers and leave under the grill or on top of a BBQ until scorching hot. Carefully pick up the scorching hot skewers and scorch the top of each nigiri to produce charcoaled lines running across the flesh. Top each nigiri with a half a teaspoon of caviar, small blobs of oroshi grated ginger and garlic and finely chopped leek.

Makes about 20 pieces

tamago omelette nigiri

see variations page 91

You tend to hear that the Japanese have no sweets, but they do. The place for sweets is with a cup of tea between meals. Thus, it is not uncommon to end a sushi dinner with a piece of sweet tamago sushi.

1 tsp sugar
30 ml (2 fl. oz) dashi (page 44)
2 tsp soy sauce
1 tsp mirin
6 eggs

vegetable oil, for frying
400 g (12 oz) shari rice (page 28)
nori sheet
wasabi

Prepare the omelette as described on page 189. Make the nigiri as described on pages 20–1. Cut a 1.25-cm (½-in) wide, 7.5-cm (3-in) long strip of nori and make a band around the centre of the tamago. This is a traditional way of securing a topping that is difficult to hold in place, and is not a sign of an amateur!

If you would like this dish to be vegetarian, make your dashi using konbu kelp and shiitake mushroom, and not katsuoboshi bonito flakes as described on page 44.

Makes about 10 pieces

salmon nigiri

see base recipe page 57

tuna nigiri
Replace the salmon with yellowfin tuna.

bass, spring onion & ginger nigiri
Replace the salmon with bass. Generally, choosing a large adult bass will provide a creamier texture. Using a flat grater, grate a 13-mm (8-in) piece of ginger; finely chop half the spring onion using, ideally, the part that moves from white to green. Place a small sprinkle of each at the centre top of the bass.

turbot, ume plum & chives nigiri
Replace the salmon with turbot. With a small teaspoon, carefully put a small blob of ume plum puree on the centre top of the turbot and top with finely chopped chives.

hamachi yellowtail & chives nigiri
Replace the salmon with hamachi, an increasingly popular, usually farmed fish in the West. The creamy texture of this fish means that little needs to be done to it. Simply top with chopped chives.

horse mackerel, spring onion & ginger nigiri
Replace the salmon with horse mackerel and top with spring onion and ginger, as in the second variation above.

variations

marinated tuna nigiri

see base recipe page 58

lemon sole in soy sauce, mirin & sake nigiri
Replace the tuna with a fillet of lemon sole. Once skinned, slice into thin, 3-mm
(⅛-in) thick strips and reduce the marinating time to 20–30 minutes.

grey mullet in soy sauce, mirin & sake nigiri
Replace the tuna with a fillet of grey mullet. Slice into thin, 3-mm (⅛-in) thick strips. Reduce
the marinating time to 20–30 minutes.

tiger prawn & shari vinegar nigiri
Replace the tuna with boiled tiger (jumbo) prawns. Marinate it in the shari vinegar mixture
used to make sushi rice (page 28).

tiger prawns in gari ginger juice nigiri
Replace the tuna with boiled tiger (jumbo) prawns. Omit the boiling water stage. Pickled gari
ginger from a Japanese supermarket comes vacuum packed in its own juices, or you can
make your own pickled ginger (page 32). These vinegary ginger juices are good to marinate
the prawns in for about 30 minutes.

mackerel nigiri

see base recipe page 61

herring in rice vinegar nigiri
Replace the mackerel with herring and shorten the marinating time to about 30 minutes.

sardines in rice vinegar nigiri
Replace the mackerel with sardines and shorten the marinating time to about 45 minutes.

aji horse mackerel in rice vinegar nigiri
Replace the mackerel with horse mackerel (*Trachurus japonicus*), a much underrated fish outside of Japan. Shorten the marinating time to about 30 minutes.

anchovy in rice vinegar nigiri
Replace the mackerel with anchovy and shorten the marinating time to about 10 minutes. If you are using tinned anchovies take care to rinse them of their salt, and remove the backbone and tail.

variations

lobster tail & yuzu mayonnaise nigiri

see base recipe page 62

tiger prawn nigiri
Replace the lobster with tiger (jumbo) prawns, prepared in the way described on page 225.

ama ebi sweet prawn nigiri
Replace the lobster with ama ebi sweet prawns. There are two commonly used prawns for ama ebi: the Alaskan pink prawns (Pandaluseous makarov) or botan prawns (Pandalus nipponensis), found more frequently off the West coast of the United States. Remove the head and shell gently so as not to break the tail, taking the intestinal tract with it. Remove any remainding intestinal tract. Soak in a bowl of salted water for 5 minutes, then rinse. Amaebi has a distinctive enough flavour, but it is nice to add a blob of mayonnaise. Wasabi mayonnaise suits these prawns better than yuzu.

scallop & shiso nigiri
Staying with the raw style of the variation above, prepare scallops in the way described on page 100. Cut a shiso leaf in half and lay it on top of the shari rice ball before topping it with the raw scallop. Again, scallops are wonderfully sweet in their own right, but a blob of wasabi mayonnaise adds another tasty dimension.

akagai red clam nigiri
Replace the lobster with akagai red clam. The part of the clam eaten here is the exterior mantle that houses the clam's body. Try to find a Japanese grocer to prepare it for you. Best eaten without mayonnaise.

variations

tea-smoked salmon & cress nigiri

see base recipe page 64

hamachi yellowtail, jalapeño & coriander salsa garnish nigiri
Replace the salmon fillet with yellowtail, and replace the wasabi mayonnaise and chives with coriander–chilli salsa.

tea-smoked salmon, soy, mirin, kimchee & shichimi 7-spice chilli pepper garnish nigiri
Combine equal portions of light soy sauce and mirin, and add a teaspoon of kimchee base. Using a pastry brush, coat the tea-smoked salmon top with the mixture and finish with a sprinkle of shichimi.

smoked salmon, cream cheese & chives nigiri
Replace the tea-smoked salmon with thinner slices of smoked salmon. Top each nigiri of smoked salmon with a blob of cream cheese that has been beaten to make it smooth, and add chopped chives.

avocado, jalapeño & coriander salsa nigiri
A delicious vegetarian alternative is to replace the tea-smoked salmon with a slice of avocado. This goes really well with the jalapeño salsa.

foie gras & pomegranate nigiri

see base recipe page 66

seared duck & chives nigiri

Prepare the duck breast in the same way as the foie gras, using a little oil to fry it. There is no need to coat the duck breast in flour. Decorate with chopped chives for more colour.

seared beef & pink peppercorn nigiri

Prepare the beef fillet the same way as the foie gras, using a little oil to fry. There is no need to coat the beef in flour. Add pink peppercorns instead of pomegranate to the sauce.

seared hamachi yellowtail & wasabi nigiri

Prepare the yellowtail fillet the same way as the foie gras, using a little oil to fry. There is no need to coat the fish in flour. Add a hint of wasabi powder instead of pomegranate to the sauce.

seared tuna, korean gochujang chilli sauce & spring onion nigiri

Prepare the tuna fillet in the same way as the foie gras, using a little oil to fry. There is no need to coat the fish in flour. Add a teaspoon of Korean chilli sauce instead of pomegranate to the sauce, and top with chopped spring onion.

ankimo monkfish liver nigiri

Prepare the ankimo, 'foie gras of the sea', as described on page 206, coating it in potato flour. Add sansho pepper to the sauce, and top with chives.

variations

yubiki scalded red snapper nigiri

see base recipe page 69

turbot, oroshi daikon white radish & yubiki nigiri
Replace the red snapper fillet with turbot and substitute the lime and sea salt garnish with grated white radish.

lemon sole, sea salt & lime yubiki nigiri
Replace the red snapper with lemon sole.

red mullet, sea salt & lemon yubiki nigiri
Replace the red snapper with red mullet. The red mullet is a beautiful example of the yubiki technique because the red scales contrast so strikingly with the white flesh. Mix the sea salt with lemon zest for the garnish.

flounder, spring onion & ginger yubiki nigiri
Replace the red snapper with flounder and top with grated oroshi ginger and finely chopped spring onion.

variations

aburi hamachi yellowtail

see base recipe page 70

tataki tuna & gochujang korean chilli mayonnaise aburi nigiri
Replace yellowtail with tuna, blowtorch and top with a dot of gochujang chilli mayonnaise (page 50).

sole, yuzukosho & oroshi daikon aburi nigiri
Replace yellowtail with sole (or another firm, white, flatfish). Top with yuzukosho (page 76).

salmon, saikyo miso & chives aburi nigiri
Replace yellowtail with salmon, blowtorch, top with saikyo miso (page 40) and blowtorch again. Garnish with chopped chives.

sea urchin uni roe & sea salt aburi nigiri
Replace yellowtail with sea urchin. Blowtorch, add a tiny sprinkle of good sea salt and secure this with a band of nori.

tofu & saikyo miso sauce aburi nigiri
Replace yellowtail with chunks of tofu cut into nigiri shapes, blowtorch and top with saikyo miso (page 40). Blowtorch again to create a classic tofu dengaku dish.

variations

grilled shishito pepper nigiri

see base recipe page 73

nimono shiitake mushroom & smoked paprika mayonnaise nigiri
Replace peppers with shiitake mushrooms. If using dried shiitake, simmer one large
mushroom for each nigiri, cooking them for a little longer than you would fresh ones.

nimono enoki mushrooms & smoked paprika mayonnaise nigiri
Replace peppers with enoki mushrooms. Simmer a small bunch of enoki for each nigiri, being
careful not to break their bases.

avocado & smoked paprika mayonnaise nigiri
Replace grilled peppers with slices of avocado; a large, sliced avocado should make five nigiri.

marinated tofu nigiri, ginger & spring onion
Replace peppers with firm tofu in soy marinade (page 58). Lightly grill 1 marinated tofu
block, cut into 1.75-cm (½-in) slices, and top with pickled ginger (page 32).

shiso & ume plum nigiri
Take one whole shiso leaf, make a nigiri sushi form, and top with a blob of tangy ume paste.

inari tofu nigiri
Replace peppers with inari tofu. Wash and cut a slice of inari tofu and top with scallion
and ginger.

variations

octopus nigiri

see base recipe page 74

octopus & nori nigiri
Plain and simple: omit the soy brushing at the end.

octopus, chilli, oroshi daikon & lime nigiri
Omit the soy, mince the daikon radish with finely chopped red chilli and lime zest for your daikon oroshi topping.

squid, ume plum & spring onion nigiri
Replace octopus with squid as prepared on page 17. Grill the squid until the surface turns opaque. Cut the squid into nigiri shapes and top with ume plum paste and chopped spring onion.

squid, chilli & lime nigiri
Replace octopus with squid as prepared on page 17. Grill the squid until the surface turns opaque. Cut the squid into nigiri shapes and top with finely chopped chilli and lime zest.

squid & shiso nigiri
Replace octopus with squid as prepared on page 17. Grill the squid until the surface turns opaque. Cut the squid into nigiri shapes, brush with the soy marinade and garnish with chopped shiso leaf.

scorched plaice nigiri

see base recipe page 76

scorched bass, daikon oroshi & yuzukosho nigiri
Replace the plaice with bass fillet.

scorched salmon & shichimi 7-spice pepper nigiri
Replace the plaice with salmon fillet, scorching for a little longer as it has a fattier, denser flesh. Sprinkle with shichimi pepper.

scorched tuna, sea salt & black pepper nigiri
Replace the plaice with tuna fillet. After scorching, simply top with crushed black pepper and sea salt.

scorched king crab & wasabi mayonnaise nigiri
Replace the plaice with meat from 1 king crab. Boil the crab and cut the shell with scissors to extract the legs in one piece. As each crab piece will form one whole nigiri, take care not to break the flesh when removing it. Secure with a strip of nori. Once scorched, top with wasabi mayonnaise (page 50).

scorched scallop & shiso nigiri
Replace the plaice with scallops as prepared on page 110. Top with torn shiso leaf.

variations

tataki beef & caviar nigiri

see base recipe page 77

tataki quail & spring onion nigiri

Prepare the basic recipe, replacing beef with a quail breast. Sear and top with finely sliced
spring onion and the oroshi grated ginger and garlic.

tataki duck & pomegranate nigiri

Prepare the basic recipe, replacing beef with a duck breast. Sear and top with oroshi daikon
grated white radish, mixed with a few pomegranate seeds and a splash of soy sauce.

chorizo & smoked paprika mayonnaise nigiri

Prepare the basic recipe, replacing beef with 1 medium link chorizo sausage, panfried and
cut into long diagonal pieces, and top the nigiri with a dab of smoked paprika mayonnaise
(page 50) and oroshi grated garlic.

tamago omelette nigiri

see base recipe page 78

tamago with adzuki bean sweet nigiri
Prepare the basic recipe, adding a tablespoon of cooked, sweetened adzuki beans to the uncooked egg mixture.

yokan adzuki bean jelly sweet nigiri
Yokan is a thick red bean paste, and makes an unconventional and sweet topping for sushi. You can buy koshian, adzuki bean paste, from Japanese grocery stores. Slice the yokan into pieces 5 cm (2 in) long, 3.75 cm (1½ in) wide, and 0.75 cm (½ in) thick, and place on top of the nigiri rice. Secure with a band of nori.

yokan aduki bean jelly & chestnut sweet nigiri
Prepare the recipe above, adding a few finely chopped boiled sweet chestnuts and ½ teaspoon honey to top the nigiri.

gunkan battleship sushi

Some ingredients are softer and more liquid than most, and these need help staying atop the rice. Hence, they are held in place by a strip of nori. The appearance of this strip resembles old battleships, and hence the name. When making gunkan, remember that moist hands are good when touching the shari rice, but it is best to have dry hands when handling the nori.

ikura salmon roe classic gunkan

see variations page 112

There are a few gunkan toppings that are seen far more often than others, and ikura is probably the most common. Bears hunting salmon in the rivers of Canada can often be seen savoring their prey's nutritious, delicious roe. Once you've tasted it for yourself, you'll know that the bears are on to something.

4 tsp salmon roe
3 tbsp soy sauce
3 tbsp sake

4 tsp shari rice (page 28)
1 nori sheet
wasabi

Place the salmon roe in a small bowl and cover with the soy and sake. Marinate in a refrigerator for at least 4 hours. Pour off the soy and sake, taking care not to break the eggs.

To create the gunkan shape, first cut the nori into 15-cm (6-in) long and 2.5-cm (1-in) wide strips (one sheet of nori will cut into 6 strips). Moisten your hands with vinegared water. Take a golf ball-sized ball of rice and shape it into an oblong with rounded edges. Dry your right hand and place a nori strip in it. With the rough side facing the rice, press the end of the nori to the rice and wrap it all around the rice ball. Crush one grain of rice and use this to paste down the overlapping ends of the nori. Daub a little wasabi on top of the rice, and add 1 teaspoon of the salmon roe, taking care not to moisten the sides of the nori.

Serve immediately, otherwise the nori becomes soggy and difficult to eat. Because of this, if you are making a selection of sushi, it is best to leave gunkan until the last. Salmon roe is already quite salty, but if you'd like to add soy sauce, pour it on top of the roe directly from a dispenser, rather than dipping the gunkan. Gunkan are usually served in pairs.
Makes 1 gunkan

aji no tataki horse mackerel gunkan

see variations page 113

Often there are smaller bits of fish fillets left over that are difficult to use in nigiri or sashimi but make perfect gunkan ingredients. They are chopped into small pieces and spooned on top of the gunkan.

1 tbsp horse mackerel fillet
1 tsp spring onion
1 tsp minced grated ginger
1 tsp ponzu sauce (page 39)

4 tsp shari rice (page 28)
nori sheet
wasabi

Prepare the horse mackerel fillet in the sanmai 3-piece method as described on page 16. It is only a small fish, but you can use the fatter parts of the fillet for nigiri sushi. Chop the smaller ends into small pieces.

The word tataki means to strike or pound, so here we have beaten, or minced, horse mackerel. Thinly slice the spring onion and mix with the horse mackerel and minced ginger along with the ponzu sauce. Make the gunkan as described on page 93, and spoon over the horse mackerel mixture. You won't need soy sauce.

Makes 1 gunkan

crab & avocado gunkan

see variations page 114

I have seen Japanese and French friends sit for hours over a plate of freshly boiled crabs, picking happily away at the flesh – slow food to be lingered over and appreciated. If you're not happy with waiting, it is easy to buy processed crabmeat, and this is fine to use in gunkan.

1 tbsp crabmeat	1 tbsp avocado
4 tsp shari rice (page 28)	soy sauce, to serve
nori sheet	

Any edible crab can be used in gunkan, though many tend to use spider crab for its sweeter flesh (there are a number of varieties of spider crab around the world, so ask your fishmonger for one with the sweetest flesh). Steam the crabs whole over a high heat for about 20 minutes (less for smaller crabs). Separate the crab body from the shell and remove the meat. Mix the brown and white crabmeat together, adjusting the ratio according to your preference.

Make the gunkan shape as described on page 93. Chop the peeled avocado into small pieces. Gently combine the chopped avocado with the crabmeat, or use decoratively fanned slices of avocado, and spoon the crabmeat onto the gunkan.

Pour the soy sauce on top of the crab directly from a dispenser rather than dipping the gunkan in a bowl of soy sauce.

Makes 1 gunkan

prawn tempura gunkan

see variations page 115

A variety of textures is an important consideration in Japanese food, and making tempura toppings for a gunkan is a tasty, though unconventional option.

1 tiger prawns
4 tsp shari rice (page 28)
nori sheet
wasabi
chilli mayonnaise (page 50)
2 tsp chopped chives

for the batter (to coat up to 30 prawns)
250 g (8 oz) plain flour plus a little extra
   for coating
1 large egg
375 ml (12 fl. oz) ice water and ice cubes
vegetable oil for deep-frying

Prepare the prawns as described on page 225. Now make the tempura batter. The secret is to not beat the batter too vigorously, so mix the flour, egg and ice water with chopsticks and leave lumps of flour unblended. You can also add ice cubes if you like.

Heat the vegetable oil in a small deep saucepan to 170°C (335°F). If you don't have a thermometer, you can test the temperature by flicking in a drop of batter. It should sink and then rise; if it just sinks it is too cool, and if it rises right away it is too hot. Coat the prawns in a little flour. Remove the excess flour, then dip it into the batter. Carefully drop it into the hot oil for about 3 minutes or until the batter has turned golden. Remove the prawns with chopsticks or a draining spoon and leave to drain on a wire rack or a kitchen towel.

Make the gunkan shape as described on page 93. Chop the prawn tempura into 2-cm (¾-in) long pieces. Spread a layer of chilli mayonnaise over the rice, and top with pieces of the prawns. Decorate with chopped chives.
Makes 1 gunkan

octopus ceviche &
red pepper gunkan

see variations page 116

South American chefs put ceviche sauces on the map, and though not at all
traditional in Japan, the slightly poached effect is delicious. Like the tataki preparation,
this sauce can be used on the thinner ends of a fish that are left over when making
nigiri or sashimi.

4 tsp shari rice (page 28)
nori sheet
wasabi
1 tbsp octopus

1 tsp chopped red pepper
2 tsp ceviche sauce (page 43)
shiso cress or mustard and cress

Make the gunkan shape as described on page 93.

Prepare the octopus as described on page 74. Dice the octopus and combine with the
chopped red pepper and the ceviche sauce.

Spoon the octopus mixture over the rice and decorate with shiso cress or mustard and cress.

Makes 1 gunkan

panfried duck, pomegranate, soy sauce & honey gunkan

see variations page 117

The pomegranate, soy, and honey sauce is somewhere in between hoisin sauce and sour cherry.

1 duck breast
salt and pepper
200 g (7 oz) yuzu mayonnaise (page 34)
3 tbsp soy sauce
1 tbsp honey

1 tbsp pomegranate seeds, reserving some
    for decoration
7 tbsp chopped chives
400 g (12 oz) shari rice (page 28)
4 nori sheets

Clean and trim the duck breast. Heat a small non-stick frying pan and, without using oil, panfry the breast skin-side down, turning it and cooking until it is golden brown on both sides. Remove from the heat, wrap in foil, and leave for 10 minutes. Remove the foil, slice into thin slices and season with salt and pepper. Bake in an oven on a high heat of 200°C/ Gas Mark 6 (400°F) for just a minute.

Combine the yuzu mayonnaise with the soy sauce, honey, pomegranate seeds and chopped chives. Make the gunkan shape as described on page 93. Spoon the yuzu mayonnaise on top of the rice. Arrange a slice of the duck breast on top and decorate with a few pomegranate seeds.

Makes 20 gunkan

uni sea urchin & burnt creamy miso mayonnaise gunkan

see variations page 118

Miso dengaku, a creamy sauce made with white miso, is perhaps best known served on aubergine. It is always a popular dish. Miso is strongly flavoured so in this recipe it is combined with a wasabi mayonnaise. You can mix and match as you like.

1 sea urchin
1 thin slice of cucumber
½ tsp wasabi mayonnaise (page 50)
½ tsp saikyo miso (page 40)

4 tsp shari rice (page 28)
1 nori sheet
shredded nori

Place the sea urchin on a thin slice of cucumber. This is to steady it whilst it is under the grill. Put it on a grill pan and spoon ½ teaspoon of wasabi mayonnaise on the left side of the sea urchin and ½ teaspoon of saikyo miso on the right. Grill until the surface turns golden brown.

Make the gunkan shape as described on page 93. Carefully lift the cucumber and urchin and place on top of the rice. Garnish with shredded nori.

Note: You can achieve the same effect using a blowtorch lightly over the topping of the mayonnaise and miso.

Makes 1 gunkan

squid with ginger, sake, soy sauce & sesame gunkan

see variations page 119

Light pan-frying is a quick and easy cooking method — particularly for shellfish and white fish — as there's no need to marinate first.

250 g (8 oz) squid tentacles
1 tbsp vegetable oil
2 tsp toasted sesame oil
2 tbsp dashi (page 44)
2 tbsp soy sauce
2 tbsp sake

1 tbsp mirin
4 tsp grated ginger
400 g (12 oz) cup shari rice (page 28)
sesame seeds
wasabi, to serve

Prepare the squid as described on page 17. You can use the body as well if you like but on a gunkan the tentacles look particularly tempting with their bright colour and curly shapes. Cut the tentacles into 2-cm (³/₄-in) cubes.

Heat the oil in a skillet and add the prepared squid. Combine the sesame oil, dashi, soy sauce, sake, mirin and ginger, and heat gently in a small saucepan. Pour it over the squid and simmer for 2–3 minutes. Drain the squid and, once cool, mix with the sesame oil. Bring the remaining liquid to a high heat to reduce.

Make the gunkan shape as described on page 93. Put the squid on top of the rice, add a light sprinkle of sesame seeds, and drizzle a little of the reduced soy mixture over the squid. There is no need to dip this gunkan in soy before eating.
Makes 20 gunkan

shiitake mushroom gunkan

see variations page 120

Shiitake mushrooms are renowned for their intense flavour and aroma and are becoming increasingly popular in the West for their good taste and health benefits. They are thought to help fight cancer and have long been used in Chinese medicine to boost the immune system. Moreover, they have nearly zero calories and plenty of vitamin D. In spite of being a classic Japanese ingredient, they are not often found in sushi.

1–2 shiitake mushrooms (dried ones are fine)
6 tbsp dashi (page 44)
1 tbsp mirin

1 tbsp soy sauce
4 tsp shari rice (page 28)
chopped chives

Rehydrate your mushrooms in a bowl of water for 30 minutes if you are using dried ones. Clean and cut off any hard part of the stem if using fresh ones.

In a small pan, combine the dashi, mirin and soy sauce, and bring to a gentle boil. Simmer the shiitake for 3 minutes or until soft and bouncy to the touch. Drain and cool. Chop into slices or chunks, as you prefer.

Make the gunkan shape as described on page 93. Arrange the mushrooms on top of the rice and add a light sprinkle of chives.

There is no need to dip this gunkan in soy before eating.

Makes 1 gunkan

scallop with shiso gunkan

see variations page 121

This is a classic combination, where the subtle balance of green in the shiso and white of the scallop appeal to the eye, and the sweet creaminess of the scallop contrasts with the fragrant sharpness of the shiso leaf.

1 scallop
4 tsp shari rice (page 28)
chopped shiso leaf

It is preferable to use live scallops in their shell for this as they are eaten raw, though you can substitute with frozen scallop meat. Extract the scallop from the shell. Remove the beard and innards and discard. Rinse the scallop in cold water and drain. Reserve the shells and scrub thoroughly.

Make the gunkan shape as described on page 93. Chop the scallop into small cubes and mix lightly with the chopped shiso leaf.

This gunkan is best eaten with a little soy sauce.

Makes 1 gunkan

variations

ikura salmon roe classic gunkan

see base recipe page 93

mentaiko pollock roe gunkan
Replace salmon roe with pollock roe, which is much smaller and is marinated in sake, soy and chilli to produce a red, smoky chilli mixture.

masago capelin roe gunkan
Replace salmon roe with capelin roe. The roe are small, and the membrane quite tough, so they give a popping sensation when chewed.

kazunoko herring roe gunkan
Replace salmon roe with herring roe. It is quite firm, with an amazingly crunchy texture.

uni sea urchin gunkan
Replace salmon roe with fresh uni. Only the gonads of the urchin are eaten in sushi. It has an extraordinary rich creaminess with an ocean-fresh scent.

caviar gunkan
Replace salmon roe with caviar. Opt for sustainably raised caviar and mix with a little wasabi.

variations

aji no tataki horse mackerel gunkan

see base recipe page 94

salmon tataki & avocado gunkan
Replace mackerel with finely chopped ends of salmon fillet mixed with one slice of avocado chopped into similar-sized pieces. Top the gunkan with the mixture and serve with wasabi mayonnaise (page 50).

tuna tataki, spring onion & wasabi mayonnaise gunkan
Replace mackerel with finely minced yellowfin tuna. Mix with 1 teaspoonful of thinly sliced spring onion and wasabi mayonnaise to top the gunkan.

plaice tataki, ume plum & chive gunkan
Replace mackerel with finely chopped ends of plaice fillet. Mix with a little ume plum puree and chopped chives to top the gunkan.

hamachi yellowtail tataki & shiso gunkan
Replace mackerel with finely chopped ends of yellowtail fillet. Mix with a little chopped shiso leaf and ponzu sauce (page 39) to top the gunkan.

ama ebi sweet prawn tataki & avocado gunkan
Prepare the sweet prawns as described on page 225, and cut into small pieces. Chop one slice of avocado into similar-sized pieces and add a little wasabi mayonnaise. Spread the mixture over the prawns.

variations

crab & avocado gunkan

see base recipe page 97

lobster & chive gunkan
Replace crabmeat with lobster as prepared on page 62. Chop into 2-cm (³/₄-in) square pieces and mix with chopped chives to top the gunkan.

prawn & yuzu zest gunkan
Replace crabmeat with prawns as prepared on page 225, and combine with the zest of yuzu (or lemon) to top the gunkan.

crabmeat & spring onion gunkan
Prepare the basic recipe, omitting the avocado and adding 2 teaspoons of finely chopped spring onion to the crab meat.

raw lobster, oroshi daikon & ponzu gunkan
Replace crabmeat with finely chopped raw lobster meat. Combine with a teaspoon of ponzu sauce (page 39) and grated daikon radish to top the gunkan.

langoustine & avocado gunkan
Replace crabmeat with boiled langoustine chopped into 1-cm (¹/₃-in) square pieces. Combine with the avocado and a teaspoon of yuzu mayonnaise (page 34) to top the gunkan.

variations

prawn tempura gunkan

see base recipe page 98

monkfish tempura, lime & sansho pepper gunkan
Replace prawns with monkfish tail. Sprinkle sansho pepper and sea salt in the flour before frying. Sprinkle over lime zest to serve.

squid tempura & chilli gunkan
Replace prawns with 15 g (½ oz) of small pieces of squid. Top with finely chopped red chilli.

lobster tempura & lemon gunkan
Replace prawns with lobster tail cut into 2-cm (¾-in) pieces and mixed with lemon zest.

scallop tempura & shiso gunkan
Omit prawns. Deep-fry a scallop. You can use the coral as well as the white meat if you like. Chop into small pieces and sprinkle with torn shiso leaf to top the gunkan.

crab claw tempura, chives & yuzu mayonnaise gunkan
Replace prawns with the meat of a crab claw. Place on top of the gunkan. Top with chives and yuzu mayonnaise.

oyster tempura & chilli gunkan
Omit prawns. Tempura one whole oyster. Place it on top of the gunkan and garnish with chopped chilli.

octopus ceviche & red pepper gunkan

see base recipe page 100

plaice ceviche & spring onion gunkan
Replace octopus with chopped raw plaice and combine with chopped chives and a spoonful of ceviche sauce to top the gunkan.

salmon, jalapeño salsa & avocado gunkan
Replace octopus with chopped raw salmon and replace red pepper with chopped avocado and a spoonful of jalapeño salsa (page 54). Combine to top gunkan.

hamachi yellowtail with jalapeño salsa & pink peppercorn gunkan
Replace octopus with chopped raw yellowtail and combine with a spoonful of jalapeño salsa (page 54), a few pink peppercorns and mustard & cress or shiso cress.

turbot ceviche with coriander & chive gunkan
Replace octopus with chopped raw turbot and combine with a spoonful of ceviche sauce and chopped coriander and chives.

cuttlefish ceviche & cucumber gunkan
Replace octopus with chopped raw cuttlefish and combine with a spoonful of ceviche sauce and a few slices of thinly sliced cucumber.

panfried duck, pomegranate, soy sauce & honey gunkan

see base recipe page 102

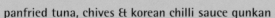

panfried tuna, chives & korean chilli sauce gunkan
Prepare the basic recipe, replacing duck with a fillet of tuna, using a little oil to fry. Make the gunkan using Korean chilli sauce (page 54), and garnish with chopped chives.

baked scallop & ponzu butter gunkan
Omit the frying stage and replace duck with 10 large scallops. Season the scallops with salt and pepper and bake at 200°C/Gas Mark 6 (400°F) for 3 minutes. Combine 4 tablespoons yuzu mayonnaise (page 34) with 2 tablespoons ponzu (page 39) and top the gunkan with shredded nori.

panfried beef with teriyaki & yuzukosho oroshi gunkan
Prepare the basic recipe, replacing duck with a tender cut of beef such as loin or rib, using a little oil to fry. Omit soy sauce, honey and pomegranate. Brush the beef with teriyaki sauce (page 36), and decorate with a blob of yuzukosho paste mixed with grated daikon white radish.

baked foie gras gunkan
Omit the frying stage and replace duck with foie gras, coated in potato flour. Season with salt and pepper and bake at 200°C/Gas Mark 6 (400°F) for 3 minutes. Omit soy sauce, pomegranate and honey and decorate with chopped mitsuba leaf (Japanese wild parsley).

variations

uni sea urchin & burnt creamy miso mayonnaise gunkan

see base recipe page 105

oyster & dengaku white miso gunkan
Replace urchin with a raw oyster. Spoon over a little saikyo miso sauce (page 40) and either grill or blowtorch until browned.

mentaiko pollock roe & creamy wasabi sauce gunkan
Replace urchin with 1 tablespoon pollock roe. Spoon over a little wasabi mayonnaise and either grill or blowtorch. Top with shredded nori.

shirako cod milt & spring onion gunkan
Replace urchin with 15 g (½ oz) shirako cod milt on a slice of cucumber. Sprinkle with chopped spring onion and spoon on a little smoked paprika mayonnaise (page 50). Then either grill or blowtorch.

octopus & dengaku white miso gunkan
Replace urchin with 15 g (½ oz) boiled octopus. Spoon over a little saikyo miso sauce (page 40) and either grill or blowtorch until browned.

duck with dengaku white miso gunkan
Replace urchin with a 15 g (½ oz) slice of duck breast, prepared as on page 102. Spoon over a little saikyo miso sauce, and either grill or blowtorch until browned.

squid, with ginger, sake, soy sauce & sesame gunkan

see base recipe page 106

razor clam with yuzu, sake, sesame & soy sauce gunkan
Prepare the basic recipe, replacing squid with 7–10 razor clams cut into
2-cm (¾-in) length pieces. Replace the ginger with yuzu juice or zest.

prawns with chilli, sake, sesame & soy sauce gunkan
Prepare the basic recipe, replacing squid with 10 large raw tiger prawns cut into
roughly three pieces each. Replace the ginger with chopped chilli.

lemon sole with ginger, sake, sesame & soy sauce gunkan
Prepare the basic recipe, replacing squid with a 325 g (10½ oz) fillet of lemon
sole, chopped into larger pieces than basic recipe and coated with potato flour
before frying to help keep its shape.

monkfish with coriander, sake, sesame & soy sauce gunkan
Prepare the basic recipe, replacing squid with monkfish. Replace the ginger with
chopped coriander.

chicken with ginger, sake, sesame & soy sauce gunkan
Prepare the basic recipe, replacing squid with chicken cut into 2.5-cm (1-in)
cubes, simmering for 4–5 minutes.

variations

shiitake mushroom gunkan

see base recipe page 109

enoki mushroom gunkan
Replace the shiitake mushrooms with enoki mushrooms and sprinkle with sesame seeds.

bamboo shoot gunkan
Replace the shiitake mushrooms with bamboo shoot. Simmer the bamboo shoot in the dashi–soy sauce mixture and sprinkle with sesame seeds.

asparagus, green bean & green pepper gunkan
Replace the shiitake mushrooms with asparagus, green beans, and green pepper; they will need less simemring time than the shiitake.

lotus root & shiitake mushroom gunkan
Prepare the basic recipe. Add lotus root chunks to the pan; add the shiitake 2 minutes later.

okra gunkan
Remove the tops and stems of the okra and replace the shiitake mushrooms with topped okra. Reduce the simmering time to 1–2 minutes. Allow 1–2 okra for each gunkan.

samphire with butter teriyaki gunkan
Replace the shiitake mushrooms with cleaned samphire. Reduce the simmering time to 1–2 minutes, and add a small knob of butter to the sauce towards the end.

scallop with shiso gunkan

see base recipe page 110

cuttlefish & shiso gunkan
Replace scallop with cuttlefish. Chop into small cubes and mix with the shiso leaf to top the gunkan.

turbot & shiso gunkan
Replace scallop with 15 g (½ oz) turbot fillet chopped into small cubes. Mix with the shiso to top the gunkan.

yellowtail & shiso gunkan
Replace scallop with 15 g (½ oz) yellowtail fillet chopped into small cubes. Mix with the shiso to top the gunkan.

scallop, ceviche & shiso gunkan
Prepare the basic recipe, adding a spoonful of ceviche sauce (page 43). Garnish with torn shiso.

hosomaki

Hosomaki, meaning 'thin roll' in Japanese, are
simple and easy to make. The hallmark of a good
maki maker is to have the filling bang in the centre
of the roll. These simple canapés look attractive at
any dinner party. If you are preparing the hosomaki
some time before you plan on eating them, be
careful that you don't roll the maki too tightly;
sushi rice swells with time, and as the nori is
absorbent, a tightly made roll will squeeze the rice
and the maki will become hard.

ume plum & cucumber hosomaki

see variations page 136

Ume plum is a quintessential Japanese fruit used as an ingredient. The Japanese plum is close to the Western apricot. The plums are pickled in salt, and later in shiso leaf, to produce an exceptionally tart pickle. They contain a lot of citric acid, which is deemed to aid digestion. Often served on a bowl of rice at breakfast, they hold a special place in Japan's culinary heart.

½ nori sheet
60 g (2 oz) shari rice (page 28)
wasabi

1 tsp ume plum puree
1 tbsp julienned cucumber

Place your bamboo rolling mat with the knotted side facing up. Place the non-shiny side of the nori facing up on your mat, with the longest edge nearest you. Dampen your hands, take the rice and shape it into a narrow log on top of the nori. Being careful to not apply too much pressure so that the grains of rice remain undamaged, evenly spread the rice outwards, leaving a gap of about 1 cm (¼ in) at the top – the side farthest away from you. Dab some wasabi in a line over the centre of the rice and spread it slightly.

With a teaspoon spread the ume plum puree over the centre of the rice and place the julienned cucumber on top of the plum. Holding on to either side of the nori, at the side nearest you, roll the mat away from you with your index fingers and thumbs. Roll tightly until the near end of the nori reaches the far edge, leaving bare the strip of rice-free nori. Cover the roll with the mat (but not the rice-free gap), press gently to shape; you can make them square or round as you like. Trim the edges; cut in half, then into 6 pieces.

Makes 1 roll, or 6 pieces

oshinko pickled daikon hosomaki

see variations page 137

Pickles and vegetables often comprise the ingredients in a hosomaki. Pickles are an essential part of a Japanese meal, and they are typically served with a bowl of rice and miso soup, signifying the end of a good dinner. Each region has its own variations of pickling, but as a rule, whilst pickles in the West are made with vinegar, which softens them, Japanese pickles tend to be crunchy as they are usually made with salt.

$1/2$ nori sheet
60 g (2 oz) shari rice (page 28)

15-cm (6-in) length Oshinko pickle
wasabi

Oshinko pickles are very traditional and are commonly found in hosomaki. You may recognise them by their bright yellow centres. You can buy oshinko but be careful to purchase a good brand, as they are often full of a whole host of additives, flavourings and colourings.

Roll the maki as described on page 123, making sure to centre the strip of oshinko.

Makes 1 roll, or 6 pieces

asparagus & bacon
teriyaki hosomaki

see variations page 138

Using just a little rice and meat is a modern interpretation of the traditional hosomaki.

1 stem asparagus
1/2 nori sheet
3 tbsp shari rice (page 28)
Japanese mustard

1 slice of thinly sliced unsmoked bacon
oil for frying
1 tsp teriyaki sauce (page 36)

Blanch the asparagus. Roll the maki as described on page 123, replacing the wasabi with Japanese mustard. Put the asparagus in the centre. Wrap the filled nori with the bacon slices and secure with cocktail sticks or skewers.

Heat the oil and lightly panfry the maki on all sides. Remove the cocktail sticks and cut into 6 pieces. Spoon a little teriyaki sauce over the pieces before serving.

Makes 1 roll, or 6 pieces

brown rice & bamboo hosomaki

see variations page 139

It is not at all common to use brown rice in sushi, but here, as with onigiri, brown rice works really well. There is less starch in brown rice, so it tends to be less sticky than white rice. (See variations for uses of other grains.) In the basic recipe you can add all kinds of different vegetables to the rice, chopping them finely.

125 ml (4 fl. oz) soy sauce
125 ml (4 fl. oz) dashi (page 44)
125 ml (2 fl. oz) sake
60 ml (2 fl. oz) apple juice or 60 g (2 oz) sugar
10-cm (4-in) piece bamboo
2 shishito pedron peppers

1 medium carrot
4 water chestnuts (tinned is fine)
400 g (16 oz) cups genmai rice (page 47)
2 nori sheets
wasabi

Combine the soy sauce, dashi, sake and apple juice in a small saucepan. Add the bamboo, shishito, carrot and water chestnuts and bring to the boil, then simmer for about 2 minutes until the liquid has nearly evaporated.

Drain the vegetables and cool. When they have cooled, chop them into small cubes and mix with the brown rice.

Roll the maki as described on page 123, but as there is no filling in this roll, take care not to press down too heavily.

Makes 6 rolls, or 36 pieces

goat's cheese, chive & walnut hosomaki

see variations page 140

Dairy is not traditionally eaten in Japan, but deep-fried Brie wrapped in nori has popped up on plenty of menus in Japan's izakaya bars recently. The combination of umami rich cheeses, such as Parmesan and Roquefort, with nori, also rich in umami, make powerful savoury flavours.

1 tsp walnuts
½ nori sheet
60 g (2 oz) shari rice (page 28)
wasabi

1 tbsp calpressi goat's cheese (or any soft goat's cheese)
1 tsp chives

Toast the walnuts in a pan, remove from heat and chop. Roll the maki as described on page 123, spreading the goat's cheese along the centre. Sprinkle the toasted walnuts and whole lengths of chive over the cheese.

Makes 1 roll, or 6 pieces

fried prawn hosomaki

see variations page 141

Try to make the maki when you are ready to eat them; they are so much nicer when the fillings are still warm.

2 ebi tiger/jumbo prawns
2.5 cm (1 in) vegetable oil for deep frying
1 tbsp potato flour

½ nori sheet
60 g (2 oz) shari rice (page 28)
wasabi

Prepare the prawns as described on page 225, but don't marinate.

Heat 2.5 cm (1 in) of good vegetable oil in a small saucepan to 175°C/Gas Mark 4 (355°F).

Dust the prawns with potato flour and deep fry for 3 to 4 minutes. Roll the maki as described on page 123, making sure to centre the prawns.

Makes 1 roll, or 6 pieces

tekkamaki – tuna hosomaki

see variations page 142

Whilst the origin of tekkamaki, the tuna sushi roll, is disputed, the commonly accepted theory is that it was designed for Go, a Japanese chess-like game, so that the players could eat without getting their hands sticky or disrupting the game.

½ nori sheet
60 g (2 oz) shari rice (page 28)

wasabi
15-cm (6-in) length raw tuna

Roll the maki as described on page 123, making sure to centre the strip of tuna. If you like wasabi, now is the time to be generous with it!

Makes 1 roll, or 6 pieces

yellowtail tempura hosomaki

see variations page 143

If you are keen on sushi for its fresh, cleansing flavours and low calorie content, then this one isn't for you! But deep-frying a whole roll provides a great contrast between hot and cold, crispy and soft – both contrasts that the Japanese celebrate in their food.

$^1/_2$ nori sheet
125 g (4 oz) shari rice (page 28)
wasabi
15-cm (6-in) length yellowtail fillet
vegetable oil, for deep-frying
shiso cress
2 tsp tempura sauce (page 55)
1 tsp grated oroshi ginger

1 tsp grated oroshi daikon white radish

batter
300 g (9 oz) plain flour, plus a little extra for
    coating
1 large egg
400 g (12 oz) iced water and ice cubes

Make the hosomaki with the yellowtail in the centre as described on page 123. When you have finished rolling it, compress each end, and dip each end into the flour. Now make the tempura batter. The secret is not to beat the batter too vigorously, so mix the flour, egg and ice water with a chopstick and leave lumps of flour unblended. You can also add ice cubes if you like. Heat the vegetable oil in a small deep saucepan to 170°C/Gas Mark 4 (340°F). Very lightly flour the outside of the hosomaki by rolling it on a floured plate. Dip the whole roll into the batter, then toss into the hot oil for around 3 minutes, or until the batter has turned golden. Remove the maki with a stainless mesh spoon and leave to drain on a wire rack or kitchen paper. Cut the maki into 6 pieces. Decorate with shiso cress. Pour the tempura sauce into a small dipping bowl, and place along side it a small plate with the grated radish and ginger, added just before dipping the hosomaki roll.

Makes 1 roll, or 6 pieces

variations

ume plum & cucumber hosomaki

see base recipe page 123

ume plum & shiso hosomaki
Prepare the basic receipe. Cut a shiso leaf in half and arrange on top.

natto fermented soybean & spring onion hosomaki
Omit the ume plum puree. Roll the maki with a heaped teaspoon of natto. Sprinkle with chopped spring onion.

natto fermented soybean & okra hosomaki
Omit the ume plum puree. Roll the maki with a heaped teaspoon of natto. Sprinkle with finely chopped okra.

ume plum & daikon white radish hosomaki
Prepare the basic recipe, replacing cucmber with a 15-cm (6-in) long strip of daikon. Roll with a teaspoon of ume plum puree.

bamboo hosomaki
Prepare the basic recipe, replacing cucmber with a strip of boiled bamboo as prepared on page 247. Sprinkle with sesame seeds.

variations

oshinko pickled daikon hosomaki

see base recipe page 125

kappamaki hosomaki
Replace oshinko with raw cucumber. Sprinkle with sesame seeds.

kanpyo pickled calabash gourd hosomaki
Replace oshinko with pickled calabash in the centre. Prepare the pickle as described on page 32, replacing ginger with calabash.

enoki mushroom hosomaki
Replace oshinko with enoki mushrooms, blanched and marinated in soy sauce and rice vinegar for 30 minutes. Top with sesame seeds.

avocado & sesame hosomaki
Replace oshinko with slices of avocado with a sprinkle of sesame seeds.

asparagus hosomaki
Replace oshinko with one blanched stem of asparagus and roll with a smear of wasabi mayonnaise (page 50).

okra & sesame hosomaki
Replace oshinko with blanched okra, marinated in soy sauce and rice vinegar for 30 minutes, and roll with a sprinkle of sesame seeds.

asparagus & bacon teriyaki hosomaki

see base recipe page 126

foie gras & asparagus hosomaki

Panfry the foie gras as described on page 66. Season with a dash each of yuzu juice and truffle oil and wrap, with the asparagus and foie gras on the inside. There is no need to fry the whole maki.

pancetta (italian bacon) & fig hosomaki

Replace asparagus with 1 whole fig, cut into quarters. Wrap the roll in pancetta slices. There is no need to fry this maki.

pancetta (italian bacon), mozzarella & chive hosomaki

Replace asapargus with pencil-sized pieces of mozzarella and roll the maki sprinkled with chopped chives. Wrap the roll in pancetta slices. There is no need to fry this maki.

marinated beef hosomaki

Prepare the basic recipe, omitting asapargus. Sear a 15 g (½ oz) slice of marbled tender beef (such as sirloin or rib-eye) in a frying pan as described on page 251, and plunge into ice water. Marinate in soy sauce and mirin for at least an hour, then cut into pencil-sized lengths and place on the inside of the roll with plenty of wasabi.

variations

brown rice & bamboo hosomaki

see base recipe page 128

brown rice, red rice, ume plum, shiso & edamame
Prepare the basic recipe, replacing half the genmai rice with red rice and cooking both together. Omit bamboo, vegetables and chestnuts. Mix rice mixture with 100 g (3½ oz) boiled, chopped edamame beans. Spread a little ume plum puree across the centre of the mixed rice, add a few torn shiso leaves and roll.

brown rice, sesame, adzuki, red rice & millet
In Japan and Japanese grocery stores, you can actually buy this mix ready to steam. If you can't find it, replace ⅓ genmai rice with red rice and ⅓ with millet, and steam together. Omit bamboo, vegetables, and chestnuts. Add 2 tablespoons tinned adzuki beans, and sprinkle with black and white sesame seeds, and roll.

brown rice, gammon, peas & carrot
Replace bamboo, vegetables, and chestnuts with 90 g (3 oz) chopped gammon, 1 medium carrot, chopped and blanched, and 60 g (2 oz) boiled peas. Mix vegetables with brown rice, sprinkle with sesame seeds, and roll.

brown rice with kinpira burdock & carrot
Omit bamboo, vegetables and chestnuts. Cook the kinpira and carrot as described on page 252. Mix 50 g (1¾ oz) finely chopped onion, rice mixture, kinpira mixture and roll.

variations

goat's cheese, chive & walnut hosomaki

see base recipe page 130

gruyère & sunblush tomato hosomkai
Replace goat's cheese with a pencil-sized stick of Gruyère. Roll with some halves of sunblush (semi-sun-dried) tomatoes. This is a classic umami-rich combination.

mozzarella & sunblush tomato hosomaki
Replace goat's cheese with a pencil-sized stick of mozzarella and roll with some halves of sunblush tomato.

roquefort & endive hosomaki
Replace goat's cheese with a pencil-sized stick of Roquefort and roll with a couple of leaves of endive.

gorgonzola & celery hosomaki
Replace goat's cheese with a pencil-sized stick of gorgonzola and roll with finely chopped celery pieces.

fried prawn hosomaki

see base recipe page 133

fried asparagus hosomaki
Replace prawns with 2 asparagus spears dipped in beaten egg before frying. Add a smear of chilli mayonnaise (page 50).

fried burdock hosomaki
Replace prawns with burdock as prepared on page 252. Fry for a little longer as burdock is quite tough. Roll with a little smoked paprika mayonnaise (page 50).

fried cod hosomaki
Prepare basic recipe, replacing prawns with a thin strip of cod, about 50 g (1³/₄ oz).

fried avocado hosomaki
Replace prawns with 2 fat pencil-sized 7-cm (2³/₄-in) lengths of avocado, chopped. Roll with smoked paprika mayonnaise (page 50).

fried sweet potato hosomaki
Replace prawns with 2 fat pencil-sized 7-cm (2³/₄-in) lengths of sweet potato, thinly sliced and dipped in beaten egg before frying. Add a smear of chilli mayonnaise (page 50).

fried courgette hosomaki
Replace prawns with 1 fat pencil sized 15-cm (6-in) length of courgette, dipped in beaten egg, before frying. Add a smear of chilli mayonnaise (page 50).

variations

tekkamaki – tuna hosomaki

see base recipe page 134

salmon hosomaki
Prepare the basic recipe, replacing tuna with a pencil-sized strip of salmon.

squid, ume plum & cucumber hosomaki
Replace tuna with squid as prepared on page 17. Add julienned cucumber and a smear of ume plum puree.

bream & shiso hosomaki
Replace tuna with bream mixed with with torn leaves of shiso.

kabayaki faux eel & cucumber hosomaki
Replace tuna with faux eel as prepared on page 222, and roll with a pencil-sized strip of cucumber.

crabstick & tobiko flying fish roe hosomaki
Replace tuna with crabsticks (sticks of surumi fish paste) sprinkled with flying fish roe.

variations

yellowtail tempura hosomaki

see base recipe page 135

green bean tempura hosomaki
Prepare the basic recipe, replacing the yellowtail with raw green beans and sesame seeds.

scallop & mitsuba tempura hosomaki
Prepare the basic recipe, replacing the yellowtail with 1 large scallop cut in to pencil-thickness shapes, and add a sprinkle of mistuba trefoil leaf, or coriander.

bass & yuzukosho tempura hosomaki
Prepare the basic recipe, replacing the yellowtail with 15-cm (6-in) lengths of a fillet of bass, and a dab of yuzukosho paste before rolling.

futomaki

Futomaki are the large rolls that are particularly
popular in the West because they lend themselves
so amiably to interpretation and creativity;
essentially, you can mix and match flavours that
inspire you.

salmon & avocado futomaki

see variations page 172

Combining fish with vegetables is the most classic form of a futomaki, and the recipe below is probably most commonly found outside of Japan.

1 sheet nori
125 g (4 oz) shari rice (page 28)
wasabi
30 g (1 oz) salmon fillet cut into two
    4 x 1-cm (1^2/$_3$ x ^{1}/$_3$-in) strips

^{1}/$_2$ large avocado cut into 10-cm (4-in) strips
1 tsp tobiko flying fish roe

Make the roll as described on pages 22–3.

Makes 1 roll, or 6–8 pieces

crispy salmon skin futomaki

see variations page 173

You won't find much cooked fish in a traditional sushi bar, but at home when you are making picnic food or a bento box for school lunch, cooked fish plays a larger role, as it often require less skill (oddly!) and stays fresh longer. In the spirit of appreciating nature's gifts and its finite resources, the skin of the salmon is surely worthy of a better end than the garbage can. Not only is it truly delicious when crisped under a grill but it is highly nutritious, as most of the omega 3 and 6 and other minerals and vitamins are found in the fatty area just under the skin.

45 g (1½ oz) salmon skin (try to leave about
    4 mm/¼ in of salmon flesh under the skin)
sea salt
1 tbsp teriyaki sauce (page 36)
1 sheet nori

125 g (4 oz) shari rice (page 28)
a few leaves of lettuce
2 tsp finely chopped spring onion
1 tsp of tobiko flying fish roe (optional)

Cover the salmon skin pieces lightly with sea salt on both sides, and place under a grill until they are crispy brown and the skin starts to bubble and darken. Set aside to cool. It should now feel nearly brittle. Cut the salmon skin into long lengths and brush with the teriyaki sauce. Make the futomaki roll with the lettuce and spring onion (and tobiko flying fish roe, if using) as described on pages 22–3.

Makes 1 roll, or 6–8 pieces

california crab, flying fish roe & avocado uramaki

see variations page 174

Uramaki rolls are made by wrapping the roll with the nori on the inside. This opens up a large range of decorative options for garnish on the rice outside. Here we use flying fish roe, but you can use different roes.

1 tbsp fresh crabmeat
½ sheet nori
125 g (4 oz) shari rice (page 28)

wasabi
½ large avocado cut into 10-cm (4-in) strips
1 tsp tobiko red flying fish roe

For the crabmeat, a ratio of 2:1 white to brown meat is nice, but if you prefer it to taste more creamy, then reduce the white meat and add more brown meat. Make the uramaki roll with crabmeat and avocado as described on pages 24–5, with tobiko red flying fish roe on the outside of the roll..

Shape into triangle shapes and arrange in a circle.

Makes 1 roll, or 6–8 pieces

panfried beef & teriyaki mustard sauce uramaki

see variations page 175

Panfrying a whole roll is another unconventional but delicious way to prepare sushi.

125 g (4 oz) shari rice (page 28)
1 tsp whole grain mustard
2 tbsp teriyaki sauce (page 36)
butter for frying
1 tsp spring onion, cut into long diagonal slices
1 tbsp green beans
½ sheet nori

1 tsp julienned carrot
2 red chillies, cut in half and deseeded, julienned into thin slices
3 tbsp fillet of sirloin beef
sea salt and black pepper
chopped chives

Mix the whole grain mustard with the teriyaki sauce and set aside. Heat the butter in a pan and panfry the spring onion and green beans very lightly (or not at all if you prefer your greens crunchier). Make your uramaki with the green beans, spring onion, julienned carrots and lengths of red chilli as described on pages 24–5. Cut the fillet of beef into long, thin slices; ideally each should be about 10 cm (4 in) in length. Arrange the slices of beef, overlapping slightly, over and around the uramaki. Sprinkle with salt and pepper. Using the same butter used to fry the green beans and spring onions, place the whole beef uramaki into the pan and fry to gently brown the beef. Add the teriyaki mustard sauce to the pan and fry for another minute. Remove the uramaki from the pan and reduce the teriyaki sauce. Wrap the beef uramaki like a sausage in a piece of clingfilm and tighten at both ends to compress and shape the roll. Cut into 6 or 8 pieces and then remove the clingfilm. Spoon a little of the reduced teriyaki mustard sauce over the pieces and top with chives.

Makes 1 roll, or 6–8 pieces

squid & mizuna wrapped in cucumber

see variations page 176

Another eye-catching method of rolling sushi is to wrap it in something other than nori. In this example we use cucumber, and the variations focus on crustaceans, cephalopods and mollusks.

10-cm (4-in) length of large cucumber
1 sheet nori
125 g (4 oz) shari rice (page 28)
wasabi
1 tsp mentaiko chilli pollock roe

30 g (1 oz) very fresh squid, cleaned and cut
    into julienne strips
2 tsp carrot, julienned
2 tsp mizuna leaves, washed and dried (use
    arugula if you can't find mizuna)

With a 15-cm (6-in) knife, firmly hold the cucumber against the knife and turn the cucumber gradually to produce one long, uniform strip. If this is too difficult (and it is quite a skill!) it is all right to leave the roll unwrapped.

For this style, use the futomaki rolling technique as described on pages 22–3. Using a teaspoon, smear on the mentaiko chilli pollock roe (if you can't find this in the Japanese supermarket, substitute with a daub of wasabi paste and tobiko flying fish roe). Arrange the julienned strips of squid, carrot and mizuna leaves. Continue rolling, but before you cut the roll, place it on top of the cucumber strip and wrap the roll once more in the cucumber. Trim the roll and cut into 6–8 pieces.

Makes 1 roll, or 6–8 pieces

softshell crab daikon wrap

see variations page 177

Lightly fried maki rolls are not traditional in Japan but have really taken hold in the West. They are best served as soon as you've made them so as to get that rare contrast in sushi between hot and cold in your mouth.

1 straight, uniform width daikon radish,
    trimmed and peeled
1 sheet nori
125 g (4 oz) shari rice (page 28)
wasabi
2 tsp tobiko red flying fish roe
chives cut into 10-cm (4-in) lengths

½ large avocado cut into 10-cm (4-in) strips
vegetable oil, for frying
1 soft shell crab
potato flour
1 tsp chilli mayonnaise, plus extra
    to serve (page 50)

Get the hard part out of the way and start with making the daikon peel. With a 15-cm (6-in) knife, firmly hold the daikon against the knife and turn the daikon gradually to produce one long, uniform strip, or use a wide vegetable peeler to peel long strips. Roll the futomaki as described on pages 22–3. Add an unbroken smear of wasabi. Using a teaspoon, spread on the flying fish roe and add the long chives and avocado on top.

Bring about 2.5 cm (1 in) of good vegetable oil in a small saucepan to 200°C (400°F). Dust the softshell crab with potato flour and deep fry for 3 to 4 minutes. Drain and squash the crab to compress it sufficiently for it to fit snugly in the roll. Add the crab to the roll whilst it is still hot. Continue rolling. Before cutting the roll, place it on top of the daikon strip and wrap the roll in the daikon. Trim the roll and cut into 6 or 8 pieces. Serve with chilli mayonnaise.

Makes 1 roll, or 6–8 pieces

tempura shishito pepper futomaki

see variations page 178

This futomaki is all about texture – the crunchiness of the pepper tempura is a contrast to the softness of the warm cheese. This is one of the those dishes best served just as soon as it is made.

8–12 shishito, or Spanish pedron, peppers
60 g (2 oz) Gruyère cheese
black pepper
chopped chives
4 sheets nori
400 g (12 oz) shari rice (page 28)

250 g (8 oz) plain flour, plus a little extra
   for coating
1 large egg
375 ml (12 oz) ice water and ice cubes
vegetable oil, for deep-frying
4 tsp runny honey

Wash and cut the tops off the shishito peppers. Reserve the tops. Sprinkle the cheese with black pepper and chopped chives and gently press the Gruyère into each pepper. Put the top of the pepper back on and secure with a cocktail stick. Make the futomaki as described on pages 22–3. Now make the tempura batter. The secret is not to beat the batter too vigorously, so mix the flour, egg and ice water with chopsticks, leaving lumps of flour unblended. You can also add ice cubes if you like. Heat the vegetable oil in a small deep saucepan to 175°C (350°F). Or you can test the temperature by flicking in a drop of batter. It should sink and then rise: if it just sinks it is too cool, and if it rises right away it is too hot. Coat the shishito in a little flour and shake off the excess. Dip the shishito into the batter, then toss gently into the hot oil for about 3 minutes, or until the batter has turned golden. Remove the shishito with a stainless steel mesh spoon and drain on a wire rack or kitchen towels. Add the shishito to the roll whilst it is still hot, and drizzle a little honey over the top. Continue rolling and cut into 6 pieces.
Makes 4 rolls, or 24 pieces

avocado & ume plum uramaki

see variations page 179

Futomaki rolls can be one of those rare treats for vegetarians tired of never-ending goat's cheese and hummus. The flavours of Japan make welcome changes as they are often unique.

$^1/_2$ sheet nori
125 g (4 oz) shari rice (page 28)
shiso cress or chopped chives
1 tsp ume plum paste

$^1/_2$ large avocado cut into 10-cm (4-in) strips
lettuce leaves
375 g ($^1/_2$ oz) nimono daikon cut into
    10-cm (4-in) lengths

Make the uramaki roll as described on pages 24–5, sprinkling the outside of the roll with shiso cress or chopped chives.

Spread the ume plum paste along the middle of the roll, add the avocado, lettuce and nimono daikon, and continue rolling.

Makes 1 roll, or 6–8 pieces

toasted tofu futomaki

see variations page 180

Smoky flavours work well in vegetable rolls. Whilst tofu is not commonly found in sushi, as a vegetarian variation it is too tasty to miss.

marinade
185 ml (6¹/₂ oz) soy sauce
125 ml (4 fl. oz) rice vinegar
125 ml (4 fl. oz) mirin

100 g (7 oz) firm tofu
2 whole shiitake mushrooms

¹/₂ red pepper
1 nori sheet
125 g (4 oz) shari rice (page 28)
1 tsp ponzu sauce (page 39)
black pepper
1 tsp spring onion, chopped

Bring the soy, mirin and vinegar gently to the boil, remove from the heat and leave to cool.

Drain the tofu and slice into 1 x 10 cm (¹/₃ x 4 in) blocks. Cut the shiitake in half. Cut the red pepper into thick long slices. Place the tofu together with the red pepper and shiitake mushrooms in the cooled marinade and soak for 30–40 minutes.

Drain and place the tofu, mushrooms and pepper on a charcoal griddle. Griddle until lightly browned. The tofu will take the longest.

Make your futomaki as described on pages 22–3, sprinkling the red pepper, shiitake and tofu with black pepper and spring onion. Dip the rolls in ponzu citrus soy to eat.

Makes 1 roll, or 6–8 pieces

honey & soy quail with fig & cucumber futomaki

see variations page 181

Far from conventional, this is a delicious example of just how far you can take sushi away from its roots.

1 large quail breast

marinade
125 ml (4 fl. oz) soy sauce
125 ml (4 fl. oz) concentrated apple juice
125 ml (4 fl. oz) sake
2 tsp oroshi grated ginger with its juice

vegetable oil, for frying
2 figs, stems removed
2 nori sheets
250 g (8 oz) shari rice (page 28)
30 g (1 oz) julienned cucumber
Japanese mustard

Debone and trim the quail breast. Place the quail in a colander and pour hot water over it. Rinse in cold water and set aside. Make the marinade of soy, apple juice, sake and ginger and pour over the quail in a flat-bottomed bowl and marinate for at least 30 minutes (overnight is okay, too). Heat the oil in a frying pan, remove the quail from the marinade and panfry for a minute. Add a little of the marinade and continue to cook on each side for another 2–3 minutes (or longer if you prefer your quail not to be pink inside). Remove from the saucepan and cut the quail into 10-cm (4-in) slices. Cut the figs in quarters. Make your futomaki as described on pages 22–3, wrapping the quail, fig and cucumber. Add on top a teaspoon of the juices left in the saucepan and serve with Japanese mustard.

Makes 2 rolls, or 12 pieces

seared beef uramaki

see variations page 182

Another unconventional maki, visually stunning with the sushi roll wrapped in a tunnel of seared beef tataki.

vegetable oil, for frying
125 g (4 oz) fillet of wagyu (or sirloin beef)
125 ml (4 oz) sake
125 ml (4 oz) dark soy sauce
1 asparagus stem
½ sheet nori
125 g (4 oz) shari rice (page 28)

Japanese mustard (comparable English or
American mustard will do)
wasabi mayonnaise (page 50)
2 tsp butter
2 tsp finely sliced spring onion or red onion
black pepper

Heat the oil in a heavy-bottomed saucepan and sear the beef until brown, about 1–2 minutes on each side. Place the seared beef in a bowl of ice water and leave for about 5 minutes. Remove and drain. The surface of the beef should be nicely browned, whilst the inside should be raw. Combine the sake and soy in a flat-bottomed bowl and marinate the beef for at least 30 minutes, or overnight if you prefer. Steam the asparagus in a colander over a saucepan of boiling water, lid on, for a minute or so, making sure it is still firm and crunchy. Remove and cool. Make the uramaki as described on pages 24–5. When flipping over the nori, smear a daub of Japanese mustard down the centre of the nori instead of wasabi. Arrange the asparagus over it and roll. Cut the marinated beef into very thin slices. On a separate piece of plastic-wrapped bamboo mat, arrange the beef slices to cover the nori sheet. Place the asparagus maki roll on top of the beef and roll again. Starting from the middle, cut into 6 equal pieces. Once cut, remove the clingfilm from each piece. Drizzle with wasabi mayonnaise and top with thinly sliced spring onion or red onion.
Makes 1 roll, or 6 pieces

seared duck & grapefruit uramaki

see variations page 183

Topping a futomaki roll with a slice of seared meat makes an attractive dish, and the texture is succulent with the seared duck and firmness of the grapefruit.

marinade
90 ml (3 fl. oz) rice vinegar
1 tbsp honey
3 tbsp mirin
200 ml (7 fl. oz) dark soy sauce

125 g (4 oz) duck breast
1/2 grapefruit

30 g (1 oz) cucumber, julienned
1/2 sheet nori
125 g (4 oz) shari rice (page 28)
chopped chives
Japanese mustard (comparable English or
    American mustard will do)
2 tsp finely sliced spring onion or red onion
red chilli

Trim the duck breast. Combine the vinegar, honey, mirin and soy in a flat-bottomed bowl and marinate the duck for at least 30 minutes, or overnight if you prefer. Remove from the marinade. Heat a pan and fry the duck breast, skin-side down, for a minute or so and turn to brown the other side. Remove from the heat and wrap in tin foil for 10 minutes. The outside should be crispy brown whilst the inside is less well cooked. Pour the marinade into the pan with the duck juices and reduce over a medium heat. Set aside and cool. Cut the grapefruit into long segments. Make the nori and shari rice following the description for uramaki on pages 24–5, with the chives on the outside of the roll. When flipped over, add a daub of Japanese mustard (instead of the wasabi) down the centre of the nori. Arrange the grapefruit and cucumber over it and roll. Starting from the middle, cut into 6 equal pieces. Remove the marinated duck from the foil and cut into thin slices. Place a slice of duck on top of each piece of maki. Decorate with thinly sliced spring onion or red onion and red chilli, and spoon over a little of the reduced marinade.

Makes 1 roll, or 6 pieces

poached bass with katsuo boshi & yuzukosho uramaki

see variations page 184

I've chosen to use bass here, but you can use any sustainably caught fish that is local to your waters. Even the fish that are traditionally not used in raw sushi such as pollock or cod can be used here, as the fish is to be cooked.

45 g (1½ oz) bass fillet
200 ml (7 fl. oz) soy sauce
90 ml (3 fl. oz) rice vinegar
90 ml (3 fl. oz) mirin
½ sheet nori

125 g (4 oz) shari rice (page 28)
a daub of yuzukosho
1 tsp mizuna
1 tsp katsuo boshi

Place the bass in a small ovenproof dish. Combine the soy, vinegar and mirin and pour over the bass. Poach in the oven, pre-heated to 175°C/Gas Mark 4 (350°F) for about 10–15 minutes, depending on the thickness of the fillet.

When cool, shred the fillet into small pieces. Make the nori and shari rice following the description for uramaki on pages 24–5, daubing a little yuzukosho on it instead of wasabi and filling the centre with shredded poached bass and mizuna leaves. Roll the finished uramaki in katsuo boshi flakes and cut into 6 pieces.

Katuso boshi looses its flaky texture very quickly when exposed to anything wet, so it is best to leave this last step to when you are ready to eat it.

Makes 1 roll, or 6 pieces

'sea chicken' tuna salad futomaki

see variations page 185

The taste of tinned tuna is so different from that of a freshly cut piece of maguro (the red meat of the yellowfin, big eye or bluefin tuna), that the Japanese refer to it as sea chicken. Traditionally, fishermen have referred to the white meat of the albacore tuna as chicken of the sea, but more recently skipjack tuna is the favoured tuna species in a tin.

30 g (1 oz) tinned tuna in water
1 tsp finely chopped onion
1 tsp red radish, sliced
1 sheet nori

125 g (4 oz) shari rice (page 28)
wasabi
2 tsp watercress

Drain the tinned tuna and combine with the onion and red radish. Make the futomaki roll with the tuna mix and watercress sprigs as described on pages 22–3.

Makes 1 roll, or 6 pieces

dragon roll prawn, salmon & avocado uramaki

see variations page 186

This recipe is inspired by the Chinese dragon boats. Although the prawn head might seem overly commanding, once you get past the peering eyes, it is actually really tasty! They are, of course, totally optional.

2 large tiger prawns
potato flour
vegetable oil, for frying
45 g (1¹/₂ oz) salmon fillet

¹/₂ avocado
¹/₂ sheet nori
125 g (4 oz) shari rice (page 28)
chilli mayonnaise (page 50)

Peel the prawns, removing the heads but being careful to leave the tails in place. Reserve the heads. To make the prawn flat, turn it onto its back and make 3 small incisions at even intervals along its centre, making sure not to cut through to the other side. Then turn the prawn onto its tummy and press gently along its spine to stretch it out a little more. Rinse, coat with potato flour, and deep-fry in a small pan of hot oil. Drain on kitchen towels. Cut the salmon into 4 thin slices. Cut the avocado lengthwise into thin slices.

Make the uramaki as described on pages 24–5, placing the prawns in the middle, with the tail popping out at the side. Arrange alternate slices of avocado and salmon slices over the uramaki. Place a piece of clingfilm over the top of the salmon and avocado and press gently into shape. Cut into 6 equal pieces and, once cut, remove the clingfilm. Decorate with the prawn heads and chilli mayonnaise.

Makes 1 roll, or 6 pieces

stained glass window futomaki

see variations page 187

This maki looks tremendous, and once you've got the hang of it, isn't as hard as it looks.

125 g (4 oz) shari rice (page 28)
30 g (1 oz) yellow masago capelin roe
30 g (1 oz) wasabi masago green capelin roe
30 g (1 oz) red tobiko flying fish roe or masago
   capelin roe

2 sheets nori, cut in to halves
400g (½ oz) tamago omelette (page 189) cut
   into a 7.5-cm (3-in) pencil shape

To begin with it is a good idea to think through what you need to do to create the effect shown in the photograph: rolls are wrapped inside one another, then cut into quarters, turned over so that the cut square edges are on the outside and curved ones on the inside, then re-shaped into one large, square maki. Use far less rice in each of the maki than you would normally use.

Divide the rice into 3 and mix each with a different-coloured roe. It is best to use masago capelin roe, as the eggs are slightly smaller. Next make the smallest, inner maki roll. Cut one half of the nori sheet into half again, and use one of the quarters. With the shortest edge nearest you, spread a thin layer of yellow masago rice evenly over the nori, then roll like a hosomaki, so that the edges of the nori only just meet, and don't overlap.

Then take a ½ sheet of nori and with the shortest side nearest you, spread over a thin layer of green masago rice, leaving about ¼ of the nori uncovered at the top, place the yellow roll on top of the green rice and roll like a hosomaki. Once rolled, cut off the uncovered nori that is sticking out.

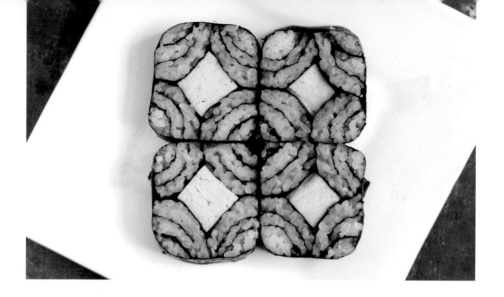

Take the last piece of ½ of nori, and with the shortest side facing, cover evenly with a thin layer of orange rice leaving a 1.25-cm (½-in) gap at the top. Place the yellow–green double roll on top of the orange rice, and roll. You should now have a colourful futomaki roll.

Leave it to set for at least 10 minutes. Then, with a sharp long knife, cut the three-colour futomaki roll in half, lengthwise. Cut each half once more lengthwise so as to make 4 long quarters. Take two quarters and flip them over so the curve edge is on the inside and the square edge on the outside. Place the piece of tamago in the centre of the curves. Complete the square by adding the remaining two quarters. Place the whole square roll on top of a ½ sheet of nori and roll one more time, to encase the inside. Gently use the bamboo mat to shape the square. Remove the mat and cut into 4–6 pieces to display your elaborate centre! *Makes 1 roll, or 4–6 pieces*

variations

salmon & avocado futomaki

see base recipe page 145

negitoro tuna belly & spring onion futomaki

Replace salmon with yellowfin or big eye tuna fillet, chopped finely almost to a paste. Mix in a touch of wasabi mayonnaise (page 50) and finely chopped spring onions.

spicy tuna & shichimi 7-spice pepper futomaki

Prepare the basic recipe, replacing salmon with 10-cm (4-in) strips of tuna, and avocado with julienned strips of cucumber and iceberg lettuce. Sprinkle over shichimi pepper and roll.

bream, ume plum & cucumber futomaki

Prepare the basic recipe, replacing salmon with 10-cm (4-in) strips of bream, and avocado with julienned strips of cucumber and frisse lettuce leaves. Replace wasabi with ume plum puree.

lemon sole & shiso futomaki

Prepare the basic recipe, replacing salmon with 10-cm (4-in) strips of lemon sole. To avocado, add a few leaves of endive and shiso.

yellowtail tuna & spicy daikon radish futomaki

Prepare the basic recipe, replacing salmon with 4-in strips of yellowtail tuna, and avocado with 1 teaspoon daikon radish with finely chopped chilli, strips of cucumber and shichimi.

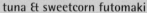

variations

crispy salmon skin futomaki

see base recipe page 146

tuna & sweetcorn futomaki
Drain a 150-g (5-oz) tin of tuna and mix with 100 g (3½ oz) sweetcorn and a level
tablespoon of wasabi mayonnaise (page 50). Make the futomaki roll with the tuna mixture,
thinly sliced red radish and sprigs of watercress.

poached salmon, asparagus & wasabi mayonnaise futomaki
Poach a few small pieces of salmon, steam a stem of asparagus and roll the futomaki with a
daub of wasabi mayonnaise (page 50).

poached salmon, cucumber & watercress futomaki
Poach a few small pieces of salmon and roll the futomaki with julienned strips of cucumber
and a sprig of watercress.

katsu deep-fried salmon & fennel futomaki
Breadcrumb and deep-fry some salmon pieces (page 234). Roll with julienned strips of
fennel, a few leaves of iceberg lettuce and a daub of tonkatsu mayonnaise (page 50).

kabayaki faux eel & cucumber futomaki
Repace salmon with kabayaki faux eel (as prepared on page 222). Roll with julienned slices of
cucumber. Best eaten when the faux eel is still a little warm from grilling.

variations

california crab, flying fish roe &
avocado uramaki

see base recipe page 149

tiger prawn & avocado uramaki
Replace crabmeat with 2 tiger prawns and replace roe with finely chopped chives.

lobster & avocado uramaki
Replace crabmeat with lobster as prepared on page 62.

scallop & avocado uramaki
Replace crabmeat with 1 large raw scallop, and replace roe with finely chopped mitsuba leaves. Roll with the avocado and a few leaves of lettuce.

tiger prawn & okra uramaki
Replace crabmeat with 2 large tiger prawns mixed with nimono-style (simmered) okra (page 73) and replace roe with sesame seeds.

squid with ume plum, shiso & caviar uramaki
Replace crabmeat with julienned strips of raw squid meat as prepared on page 17. Replace roe with caviar, and roll using a smear of ume plum and a scatter of torn shiso leaves.

tiger prawn, salmon, cream cheese & avocado uramaki
Replace crabmeat with 1 tiger prawn and 1 tablespoon of salmon, a smear of cream cheese and a sprinkle of chopped chives. Replace roe with black sesame seeds.

variations

panfried beef & teriyaki mustard sauce uramaki

see base recipe page 150

panfried duck, green beans, carrot, chilli & spring onions uramaki
Prepare the basic recipe, replacing beef with slices of duck.

panfried beef, asparagus, burdock, chilli & watercress uramaki
Prepare the basic recipe, replacing green beans with asparagus and the carrot with kinpira burdock (page 252). Use watercress to add sharpness instead of spring onion.

panfried tuna, green beans, carrot, chilli & spring onion uramaki
Prepare the basic recipe, replacing beef with 0.5-cm ($\frac{1}{4}$-in) thick slices of tuna.

panfried duck, green beans, daikon radish, sesame seeds & spring onion uramaki
Prepare the basic recipe, replacing beef with duck. Add julienned daikon instead of carrot and sesame seeds instead of chilli.

panfried tuna with wasabi mayonnaise uramaki
Prepare the basic recipe, replacing beef with 0.5-cm ($\frac{1}{4}$-in) thick slices of tuna; replace the green beans with cos lettuce, spread with a little wasabi mayonnaise.

panfried duck, cucumber, spring onion & carrot with hoisin sauce uramaki
Prepare the basic recipe, replacing beef with duck. Add julienned cucumber and spring onion along with the carrot and spread a little hoisin sauce.

variations

squid & mizuna wrapped in cucumber

see base recipe page 152

octopus, cucumber & spring onion futomaki wrap
Replace squid with boiled octopus as prepared on page 74. Add long strips of cucumber and chopped spring onion to the roll. Wrap with a film of daikon radish.

tiger prawns, green beans & smoked paprika mayonnaise futomaki wrap
Replace squid with prawns as prepared on page 225. Roll with 10 g (¹⁄₃ oz) blanched green beans and add a teaspoon of smoked paprika mayonnaise (page 50), wrap with cucumber.

scallop & shiso futomaki wrap
Replace squid with raw scallops as prepared on page 110. Add some torn shiso leaves to the roll. Add a teaspoon of ponzu sauce and wrap in cucumber.

lobster & yuzu mayonnaise futomaki wrap
Replace squid with lobster as prepared on page 62. Add lettuce leaves and a teaspoon of yuzu mayonnaise (page 34) and wrap with cucumber.

tiger prawns & yuba with sweet chilli mayonnaise futomaki wrap
Replace squid with prawns as prepared on page 225. Pat dry 2 strips of yuba tofu skin strips, which in the standard form are around 5 x 7.5 cm (2 x 3 in). Spoon over a teaspoon of sweet chilli mayonnaise and wrap in radish.

softshell crab daikon wrap

see base recipe page 154

prawns, avocado & chilli mayonnaise futomaki wrap
Replace crabmeat with 2 fried tiger prawns and roll with avocado, fish roe and lettuce.

lobster, avocado, wasabi mayonnaise & caviar futomaki wrap
Replace crabmeat with 200 g (7 oz) fried lobster meat. Roll with cos lettuce, a sprinkle of shiso cress or mustard and cress, a teaspoon of wasabi mayonnaise and a teaspoon of sustainably raised caviar or black flying fish roe.

squid, mizuna, chilli, sea salt & lime futomaki wrap
Replace crabmeat with 200g (7 oz) raw squid cut into even pieces. Roll with mizuna, chopped red chillies, zest of lime and a sprinkle of sea salt.

oyster & yuzu mayonnaise futomaki wrap
Replace crabmeat with 2 fried oysters. Roll with lettuce and a teaspoon of yuzu mayonnaise (page 34).

variations

tempura shishito pepper futomaki

see base recipe page 156

pumpkin–burdock tempura & sesame dressing futomaki
Replace pepper with 60 g (2 oz) pumpkin and 60 g (2 oz) burdock, each cut into 0.5-cm
(⅓-in) thick slices. Add a little iceberg lettuce and evenly spread a teaspoon of sesame
dressing (page 53) over the vegetables before rolling.

avocado & smoked paprika mayonnaise futomaki
Replace pepper with avocado and add a teaspoon of smoked paprika mayonnaise (page 50)
before rolling the maki.

courgette flower, burrata cheese & honey futomaki
Stuff a courgette flower with burrata cheese and complete the roll with black pepper
and honey.

shishito pepper stuffed with gorgonzola cheese & honey futomaki
Stuff the shishito pepper with Gorgonozola cheese and complete the roll with a sprinkle of
toasted hazelnuts and honey.

variations

avocado & ume plum uramaki

see base recipe page 157

shiso & cucumber uramaki
Omit avocado and roll with shiso leaf, torn with your fingers, julienned strips of daikon and cucumber and a couple of lettuce leaves. Replace shiso cress with chopped parsley.

pickled ginger, avocado & red pepper uramaki
Prepare the basic recipe, adding pickled ginger (page 32), 10-cm (4-in) strips of red pepper, julienned carrot and cucumber, lettuce leaves and a sprinkle of sesame seed. Use chopped chives on the outside.

burdock & carrot uramaki
Omit daikon and avocado, and roll using the recipe on page 252. Use sesame seeds on the outside.

purple sprouting broccoli & sesame uramaki
Omit daikon and avocado, and roll with a couple of sprigs purple sprouting broccoli, blanched, a teaspoon of sesame dressing (page 53), raw spinach leaves and julienned carrot.

toasted tofu futomaki

see base recipe page 158

toasted tofu & cucumber futomaki
Prepare the basic recipe, and roll with julienned cucumber and a sprinkle of sesame seeds.

toasted tofu, sunblush tomato, pine nuts & basil futomaki
Prepare the basic recipe and add a couple of sunblush tomatoes, with some cut in half, a few pine nuts and some torn leaves of basil. Serve with yuzu mayonnaise (page 34).

tamago sweet omelette, shiitake mushroom, bamboo shoot & watercress futomaki
Prepare the basic recipe, omitting red pepper and replacing tofu with shiitake and pickled calabash (page 49). Add to the roll a 10-cm (4-in) slice of the sweet omelette, strips of bamboo shoot (either from a tin or vacuum packed) washed and drained well and some watercress leaves.

tamago sweet omelette, carrot, green bean & inari futomaki
Prepare the basic recipe, replacing tofu with green bean and carrot. Add to the roll strips of tamago omelette and inari tofu (fried tofu skin), sprinkle with sesame seeds.

enoki mushroom, tamago sweet omelette, mizuna & yuba futomaki
Prepare the basic recipe, replacing tofu with enoki mushrooms and lightly grill. Add to the roll a strip of yuba tofu skin, tamago sweet omelette and a few mizuna leaves.

variations

honey & soy quail with fig & cucumber futomaki

see base recipe page 161

seared quail & chestnut futomaki
Prepare the basic recipe, adding pieces of boiled chestnut to the pan whilst frying the quail.
Roll with julienned cucumber.

seared duck, spring onion & red chilli futomaki
Prepare the basic recipe, replacing quail with duck breast. Roll with julienned cucumber,
chopped spring onion, julienned carrots and chopped red chilli.

panfried chorizo & green & yellow pepper futomaki
Replace quail with chorizo, cut into 10-cm (4-in) lengths and halved. Omit figs, and
cucumbers. Make marinade, but omit marinating stage. Cut a green and yellow pepper into
long slices and fry briefly in the marinade sauce with the chorizo. Serve with smoked paprika
mayonnaise (page 50).

gyoza dumplings, mizuna & daikon futomaki
Gyoza – pork and cabbage dumplings – can be found in most Japanese grocery stores. Steam
the gyoza. Omit the marinating stage. Add a drop of marinade sauce to a frying pan and
panfry the gyoza for a couple of minutes. Roll with mizuna and julienned daikon.

seared beef uramaki

see base recipe page 162

kabayaki faux eel, cucumber & avocado uramaki

Make the faux eel using the recipe on page 222. Make the inside roll using the faux eel and julienned cucumber. Make the outside wrap with finely sliced avocado. Spoon over a little faux eel sauce and top with pink peppercorn.

foie gras poached nashi pear, umeshu plum wine & cucumber uramaki

Cut 90 g (3 oz) foie gras liver into 2-cm (¾-in) thick slices. Coat with potato flour, fry until golden brown and drain on kitchen towels. Add equal parts soy, rice vinegar and umeshu plum wine to the saucepan and heat over high heat. Add 1 nashi pear and poach until soft but still crunchy. Remove pear and reduce remaining liquid. Add splash of white truffle oil and a few pink peppercorns. Roll with the foie gras and nashi pear on the inside. Make the outside using thinly sliced cucumber. Cut and top with fried leeks and a little remaining liquid.

halloumi cheese, grilled shishito pepper & pancetta uramaki

Omit beef, asparagus and wasabi mayonnaise. Brush 15 g (½ oz) each halloumi and pepper, cut into 10-cm (4-in) strips, with a mixture of soy and sake and grill. Roll using halloumi and pepper on the inside and pancetta slices on the outside.

mozzarella & smoked salmon uramaki

Omit beef, asparagus and wasabi mayonnaise. Roll using mozzarella, chopped chives and lettuce leaves on the inside and slices of smoked salmon on the outside.

seared duck & grapefruit uramaki

see base recipe page 164

beef, fig & green bean uramaki
Prepare the basic recipe, replacing duck with marinated beef fillet. Assemble the inside of the uramaki with blanched green beans and slices of raw fig, and the outside with chopped chives. Top each piece of maki with a slice of seared beef and some thinly sliced onions.

chicken, yuzukosho & spinach uramaki
Prepare the basic recipe, replacing duck with marinated thigh of chicken. Make the inside roll with a daub of yuzukosho and spinach leaves, and the outside with shiso cress. Top each piece of maki with a slice of the chicken, and decorate with shisho cress or mustard and cress.

gammon, pineapple & cress uramaki
Prepare the basic recipe, replacing duck with a marinated piece of gammon. Make the inside roll with pineapple and cucumber, and the outside with shiso cress or mustard and cress. Top each piece of maki with a slice of gammon, and sprinkle with black pepper and finely sliced red chilli.

poached bass with katsuo boshi & yuzukosho uramaki

see base recipe page 166

cod, mizuna & katsuo boshi uramaki
Replace bass with cod or any sustainably caught local whitefish available to you.

tuna, cucumber & spicy flying fish roe uramaki
Replace bass with tuna, and mizuna with cucumber. Substitute the outside katsuo boshi for a mixture of flying fish roe and shichimi pepper.

shellfish mix with mizuna & katsuboshi uramaki
Replace bass with a mixture of shellfish – clams, scallops, mussels and oysters.

smoked haddock, mizuna & prosciutto uramaki
Replace bass with smoked haddock. Substitute the outside katsuo boshi for flecks of chopped prosciutto ham.

poached monkfish, cucumber & prosciutto uramaki
Replace bass with poached monkfish, and mizuna with cucumber. Substitute the outside katsuo boshi for flecks of chopped prosciutto ham.

'sea chicken' tuna salad futomaki

see base recipe page 168

sea chicken tuna salad & sweetcorn futomaki
Replace red radish and watercress with sweetcorn.

sea chicken tuna salad & tomato futomaki
Replace red radish and watercress with chopped tomato.

sea chicken tuna salad & jalapeňo futomaki
Replace red radish, onion and watercress with chopped jalapeňo.

sea chicken tuna salad, red kidney beans & green pepper futomaki
Replace red radish, onion and watercress with kidney beans and chopped green pepper.

sea chicken tuna salad & black olive futomaki
Replace red radish, onion and watercress with chopped black olives.

dragon roll prawn, salmon & avocado uramaki

see base recipe page 169

faux eel, salmon & avocado dragon roll
Replace prawns with faux eel, as prepared on page 222.

prawn & avocado dragon roll
Butterfly the prawns to make a wider shape. Make the inside roll using julienned carrot and lettuce. Wrap with slices of avocado and boiled prawns.

tuna & avocado dragon roll
Make the inside roll using julienned carrot and lettuce, and wrap with slices of avocado and tuna.

faux eel, cucumber & avocado dragon roll
Replace prawns with faux eel, as prepared on page 222 and wrap with varying shades of green using thinly sliced avocado and cucumber.

tuna & avocado dragon roll
Make the inside roll using watercress and prawn, and wrap with slices of avocado and tuna.

stained glass window futomaki

see base recipe page 170

soboro stained glass window futomaki
Prepare the basic recipe, replacing roe with a ground meat or fish called 'soboro'. You can buy this in Japanese supermarkets, but beware, often they are just sugar and colour additives. Replace the tamago with your favourite white fish.

salmon & caviar stained glass window futomaki
Prepare the basic recipe, making the three different-coloured rice using caviar or black herring roe, plain white rice and green masago with a band of bright orange raw or smoked salmon.

saintly vegetarian stained glass window futomaki
Prepare the basic recipe, making the three different-coloured rice using black sesame seeds, the purple of ume plum furikake seasoning (which can be purchased from most Japanese supermarkets) and finely chopped green shiso leaves mixed with the rice. Your centre can be made with a band of green cucumber or yellow oshinko pickle.

sashimi

Sashimi, put simply, is freshly cut slices of uncooked fish, and it harnesses the natural good flavour of the ingredients. Although the sushi looks simple, it is absolutely true that sashimi cut by chefs who possess good knife skills, and understand the proper treatment of fish, produce sashimi with a superior and fresher taste. It is all quite subtle, but you will recognise it when you experience it.

tamago sweet omelette sashimi

see variations page 209

Sushi, being based on raw ingredients, has always been hazardous to the tummy, so some say that a sushi chef's skills should be tested on the quality of his tamago sweet omelette.

1 tsp sugar	1 tbsp mirin
60 ml (2 fl. oz) dashi (page 44)	6 eggs
30 ml (1 fl. oz) soy sauce	vegetable oil, for frying

Dissolve the sugar in the dashi, soy, and mirin. Lightly beat the eggs with a fork and combine them with the dashi mixture. Heat the pan (ideally a square one, as is conventional in Japan, though a round pan will suffice) and very lightly brush on the oil. Then pour $\frac{1}{3}$ of the omelette mix onto the pan, tilting it back and forth so as to cover the base with a thin layer of egg. Cook on medium heat until the edges are a little crisp, but the middle remains soft and runny. Then, with chopsticks or a spatula, fold the omelette in half and then into a quarter, and move it to the edge of the pan. Next pour another $\frac{1}{3}$ of the omelette mixture into the pan, lifting up the folded egg to allow the new egg mixture to run underneath it. Once cooked, this second omelette should be folded in half, then into a quarter, on top of the first, folded omelet. Repeat this process with the last $\frac{1}{3}$ of the egg mixture, folding it for the last time. Remove this solid block of omelette from the pan and allow to cool before cutting. (If a round pan was used, trim off the round edges to make a perfectly square block of omelette.)

Tamago may be served as sashimi, with no rice, and cut diagonally. Eat with soy sauce and perhaps a little daikon oroshi, grated radish.

Makes 3 portions

whitefish sashimi of red mullet, leek & ginger oroshi

see variations page 210

Traditionally, whitefish such as bass and snapper were the prized fish to eat, with salmon becoming popular only with the advent of salmon farms in the 1990s, and tuna only since the 1920s. Before then it was considered only fit for cat food! Westernisation of the Japanese diet perhaps can account for the recent enjoyment of fattier fish.

1 whole red mullet, weighing at least 800 g (28 oz) (a smaller and therefore sexually immature fish should be avoided)

200 g (7 oz) tsuma daikon white radish
5 tsp grated ginger
5 tsp finely chopped leek

Prepare the red mullet fillet as described on pages 16–17. To cut the fillet into sashimi slices, using a super-sharp knife, cut straight down across the grain, drawing the knife towards you. Start at the far end of the fillet and begin with the heel of the knife, drawing it down and upwards as you cut through the flesh. The slices should be very thin and weigh about 10 g (⅓ oz) each. This is thinner than the cut for a softer fish such as salmon or tuna. Arrange the shredded daikon on a plate and stack up the sashimi slices on top of it. Using a teaspoon, daub a little of the grated ginger on top of every other slice of mullet and decorate with chopped leek.

Makes 1 portion

hamachi yellowtail sashimi, herb ceviche sauce & ponzu olive oil

see variations page 211

Softer, fattier fish like yellowtail can take the more robust, intense flavourings and sauces, and the creaminess of hamachi yellowtail goes well with this ceviche-style sashimi.

150 g (5 oz) hamachi yellowtail fillet
a small amount daikon tsuma (page 27)
125 ml (4 fl. oz) ceviche sauce (page 43)
2 tsp finely chopped flat parsley
2 tsp finely chopped coriander
1 tsp grated oroshi daikon mixed with a drop of
    soy sauce

shiso cress
1 red jalapeño, cut into thin slices
2 tbsp ponzu sauce (page 39)
2 tbsp olive oil

Yellowtail are large fish, and you are unlikely to come across whole fish outside of Japan. Cut your yellowtail fillet into slices as described on page 18. Combine the ceviche sauce with the finely chopped parsley and coriander. Pour a little of this ceviche herb sauce on the centre of the plate, and then arrange the shredded daikon directly on top of it. Arrange the fish slices as you like around the daikon. Top each slice of fish with a spot of grated oroshi daikon with soy, a leaf of shiso cress and a thin slice of red jalapeño.

Mix the ponzu and olive oil together and drizzle over the yellowtail just before serving.

Makes 1 portion

marinated sashimi of mackerel, spring onion & oroshi ginger

see variations page 212

When mackerel is in season (generally the warmer months in the northern hemisphere, and July to October in the southern hemisphere) the high oil content in the flesh means that it is quick to deteriorate. Because the flesh of the mackerel is tender and disintegrates easily, when filleting the fish try to cut it cleanly with as few knife strokes as possible. This will help keep the flesh from oxidisation and the texture firm.

200 g (7 oz) marinated mackerel fillet (page 61)
200 g (7 oz) tsuma daikon white radish
(page 27)
lemon slices

5 tsp oroshi grated ginger
7 tbsp chopped spring onion
wasabi

Use the marinated mackerel as described on page 61. Arrange the tsuma daikon on a plate and ring the sashimi slices around the top of it. Insert a small slice of lemon between each slice of mackerel. Using a teaspoon, spoon a little ginger oroshi on top of every other slice of mackerel. Decorate with spring onion.

Makes 1 portion

usuzukuri thinly sliced turbot, ponzu, oroshi daikon & shiso cress

see variations page 213

Flatfish are often finely sliced to showcase their translucent flesh and the fresh, firm texture. Usuzukuri is usually served with the classic citrus soy sauce, ponzu.

1 turbot
2 tsp daikon oroshi grated white radish
3 tbsp ponzu sauce (page 39)

4 tsp shiso cress (most small leaves or sprouts work here)
1 lemon, cut into thin slices

You probably won't know how your turbot was caught, but try to choose a gill-netted or line-caught one, as a trawl-caught fish will have battered and bruised flesh. Ideally, your turbot will have been killed quickly and have had the blood drained out, providing reduced opportunity to contaminate the glassy white flesh.

Fillet the turbot as described on page 18 of the introduction for 5-piece filleting.

With a super-sharp knife, cut the fillet into paper-thin slices with the technique described on page 190; the idea is that they will be thin enough to see through. Once you have enough slices to fill a plate, arrange them as you like. Place the daikon oroshi on the overlapping fish slices and drizzle the ponzu sauce over the top of the grated radish. Sprinkle with shiso and decorate with lemon slices.

Serve the rest of the ponzu sauce in a small dipping bowl so that when eating you can pick up each 'petal' and dip it lightly into the ponzu.
Makes 1 portion

aburi salmon sashimi ceviche & truffle olive oil

see variations page 214

Aburi simply means to scorch, and it is a technique used to firm up a fish on the outside. Traditionally this would have been achieved using a charcoal grill.

150 g (5 oz) salmon fillet
sea salt and black pepper
60 ml (2 fl. oz) ceviche sauce (page 43)
2 tsp daikon oroshi grated white radish
1 tsp finely chopped chives

a splash of truffle oil
2 tbsp olive oil
mustard & cress or shiso cress
daikon white radish curls

Cut the salmon fillet into slices as described on page 18 of the introduction on cutting large fish. Sprinkle the fillet with sea salt and black pepper. Blowtorch the fillet enough to lightly brown the surface. (Or panfry in butter if you don't have a blowtorch.)

Cut the salmon into 1-cm (¼-in) slices. Arrange them as you like on a serving dish. Combine the ceviche sauce with the grated white radish and chopped chives. Spoon a teaspoon of ceviche mixture on top of the salmon, followed by a splash of truffle oil. Truffle oil is very pungent, so use it sparingly. Drizzle the olive oil over the salmon just before serving. Decorate with shiso cress or mustard and cress, and daikon curls.

Makes 1 portion

sesame-encrusted salmon sashimi & spicy korean chilli dressing

see variations page 215

Seared sashimi is a firm favourite in modern Japanese cooking, and the seared fattier fish are robust enough to support the strong flavour of a spicy chilli dressing.

150 (5 oz) salmon fillet
sea salt
black pepper
30 g (1 oz) mixed black and white sesame seeds
vegetable oil, for frying

125 ml (4 oz) Korean chilli sauce (page 54)
30 g (1 oz) micro greens
shiso cress

Prepare the salmon fillet as described in the introduction on page 18. Rub the fillet with salt and black pepper. Roll in the sesame seeds so that the outside is fully coated. Heat the oil in a frying pan and panfry the salmon for about one minute on each side. Remove from the heat.

When cool, slice the salmon into thick slices of about 25 g (¾ oz) each. Pour the Korean chilli sauce onto a serving plate. Arrange the salmon slices on top of the sauce, and decorate with micro greens and shiso cress.

Makes 1 portion

squid sashimi & ikura salmon roe

see variations page 216

The notion of eating raw cephalopods conjures up images of chewy, fishy, slimy things, but in fact, the opposite is true. Squid and octopus eaten raw taste of the sweetness of the sea, and their texture has a kind of crunch to the bite.

4 tsp ikura salmon roe
3 tbsp sake
3 tbsp soy sauce
150 g (5 oz) squid fillet

wasabi
30 g (1 oz) of wakame and daikon tsuma
(page 27)

Place the salmon roe in a small bowl and cover with the sake and soy. Leave in a refrigerator for at least 4 hours to marinate. Pour off the soy and sake, taking care not to break the eggs.

Prepare the whole squid as described on page 17. Place the squid fillet on a chopping board and slice into thin julienned strips. This cutting enhances the texture when in the mouth. Arrange the julienned squid on a plate, top with a teaspoon of salmon roe. Serve with wakame and daikon tsuma and, in a separate dish, a little wasabi mixed with soy sauce.

Alternatively, you can make a roll of squid with something colourful such as cucumber or a shiso leaf. Prepare a 10-cm (4-in) square fillet of squid, and make diagonal scores on one side of the flesh, taking care not to cut through it. With a 15-cm (6-in) knife, firmly hold a 10-cm (4-in) length of cucumber against the knife and turn the cucumber gradually to produce one long, uniform strip. Cover the squid with the unbroken strip of cucumber, and roll as you might a maki. Cut into 2-cm (³/₄-in) wide slices.

Makes 1 portion

octopus sashimi, teriyaki & sesame

see variations page 217

Sashimi usually denotes raw fish, but cooked octopus, squid, prawns or scallops can be made into sashimi-style dishes.

150 g (5 oz) octopus tentacle ends
45 g (1½ oz) julienned cucumber
2 tbsp teriyaki sauce (page 36)

black sesame seeds
coriander leaves

Prepare the octopus as described on page 74. As the best use for the thick parts of the tentacles is in nigiri sushi, it is okay to use the smaller ends of the tentacles in this recipe.

Place the julienned cucumber on a plate, arrange the octopus on top, and spoon over it a teaspoon of teriyaki sauce. Sprinkle sesame seeds and coriander leaves. (Or you can make little fans with the cucumber as shown in the picture, adding a more decorative touch.)

Makes 1 portion

ankimo monkfish liver

see variations page 218

There are plenty of things that come out of our sea that we outside of Japan tend to discard, and monkfish liver is just one example. In Japan they are described as the 'foie gras of the sea', and indeed, they are not dissimilar.

1 monkfish liver	1 tsp. ceviche sauce (page 43)
1 l (32 oz) water	1 tsp. caviar
30 g (1 oz) salt	

As always, make sure that your fishmonger is certain that the monkfish liver is fresh. Remove blood vessels and the membrane from the outside with a small knife. Soak the liver in salted water for about 30 minutes. You may need more than the one litre if the liver is large.

Pat dry. Put the liver on a piece of clingfilm and roll it into a cylindrical shape. Pierce a few holes in the clingfilm. Next, wrap the liver in tin foil. Tighten the liver-sausage shape at both ends, then wrap it in a bamboo maki rolling mat and secure with a rubber band. Steam in a colander over boiling water for 45 minutes.

Pour the ceviche sauce onto a plate. Once cool, cut the sausage-shaped liver into 2.5-cm (1-in) thick slices and arrange on top of the sauce. Spoon a teaspoon of caviar on top.

Makes 1 portion

korean-style sashimi & korean chilli sauce

see variations page 219

Korea is another country that enjoys serving fish in its raw state, but consistent with traditional Korean cuisine, they tend to add more flavour in the form of punchy chilli and garlic. In addition, they add plenty of vegetables, which are often lacking on restaurant menus in Japan, although at home the Japanese eat a wide variety of vegetables.

30 g (1 oz) salmon fillet
30 g (1 oz) tuna fillet
30 g (1 oz) whitefish, such as bass fillet
60 g (2 oz) shari rice (page 28)
2 tsp red cabbage, finely sliced

2 tsp tsuma daikon white radish
½ tsp micro greens
shiso cress
4 tsp Korean chilli sauce (page 54)

Chop each of the fish fillets into small cubes. Place a ball of shari rice in the centre of the bowl and arrange the red cabbage slices, shredded white radish and micro greens around it in a circular pattern. Place the three kinds of fish between the vegetables.

Decorate with micro greens and shiso cress. Serve the Korean chilli dressing in a pouring vessel so that it can be added to the dish as desired.

Makes 1 portion

variations

tamago sweet omelette sashimi

see base recipe page 189

tamago with brown prawns
Prepare the basic recipe, adding 50 g (1¾ oz) small, raw brown prawns to the egg mixture before cooking.

tamago with shiitake mushroom
Prepare the basic recipe, adding 50 g (1¾ oz) shiitake mushrooms, rehydrated in dashi and soy and chopped, to the egg mixture before cooking.

tamago, mitsuba & halloumi
Prepare the basic recipe, adding chopped halloumi cheese and mitsuba leaf or chives to the egg mixture before cooking.

tamago & green pepper
Prepare the basic recipe, adding chopped raw green pepper to egg mixture before cooking.

tamago with gammon
Prepare the basic recipe, adding small pieces of chopped ham to the egg mixture before cooking.

tamago & chestnut
Prepare the basic recipe, adding chopped re-boiled chestnuts to egg mixture before cooking.

variations

whitefish sashimi of red mullet, leeks
& ginger oroshi

see base recipe page 190

lemon sole, ginger oroshi & leeks
Prepare the basic recipe, replacing mullet with sole. You might want to fillet gomai 5 fillets rather than sanmai 3 fillets as described on page 18, if it is a large sole.

john dory, ikura salmon roe & chives
Prepare the basic recipe, replacing mullet with John Dory. Replace leeks and ginger oroshi with salmon roe and chopped chives.

red snapper & ume plum
Prepare the basic recipe, replacing mullet with red snapper. Serve on a bed of tsuma, shredded cucumber and daikon, with a daub of ume plum on each slice of snapper. Omit leeks and ginger oroshi.

dover sole & caviar
Prepare the basic recipe, replacing mullet with dover sole. You might want to fillet gomai 5 fillets rather than sanmai 3 fillets as described on page 18, if it is a large sole. Decorate with caviar.

hamachi yellowtail sashimi, herb ceviche sauce & ponzu olive oil

see base recipe page 193

salmon sashimi herb ceviche, daikon & ponzu olive oil
Prepare the basic recipe, replacing yellowtail with salmon slices.

tuna sashimi herb ceviche, shallot & ponzu olive oil
Prepare the basic recipe, replacing yellowtail with tuna, and the centre daikon tsuma with thinly sliced shallot.

scallop sashimi, jalapeño salsa, daikon & lime olive oil
Prepare the basic recipe, replacing yellowtail with raw scallop sashimi slices, omitting the ponzu. Drizzle the scallop with a little lime juice and olive oil. Replace the herb ceviche with jalapeño salsa (page 54).

ama ebi sweet prawn sashimi, jalapeño salsa, daikon & lime olive oil
Prepare the basic recipe, replacing yellowtail with raw ama ebi, omitting the ponzu. Drizzle the prawns with a little lime juice and olive oil. Replace the ceviche with jalapeño salsa (page 54).

marinated sashimi of mackerel, spring onion & oroshi ginger

see base recipe page 194

vinegared sardine sashimi

Prepare the basic recipe, replacing mackerel with sardines and shortening the marinating time by 45 minutes. Take time to cut the diagonal slices in the sardine flesh to reveal the contrasting redder flesh below. Top with chopped spring onion.

vinegared herring sashimi

Prepare the basic recipe, replacing mackerel with herring. Top with chives and shiso cress.

aji no tataki horse mackerel sashimi

Prepare the horse mackerel as described on page 94 and mix with ponzu sauce and chopped spring onion.

tororo mountain yam potato & marinated tuna sashmi

Prepare the basic recipe, replacing tsuma with julienned slices of a large, 15-cm (6-in) chunk of Japanese mountain yam potato, or nagaimo. Add 50 g (1³⁄₄ oz) tuna, cubed and marinated with sweet soy marinade (page 222) rather than the vinegar, and serve with chopped spring onion.

variations

usuzukuri thinly sliced turbot, ponzu, oroshi daikon & shiso cress

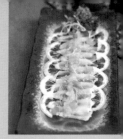

see base recipe page 196

lemon sole usuzukuri sashimi
Prepare the basic recipe, replacing turbot with lemon sole.

wrasse usuzukuri sashimi
Prepare the basic recipe, replacing turbot with wrasse prepared in the 3-fillet method described on pages 16–17.

seared beef usuzukuri sashimi, nashi pear & tamari sesame oil dressing
Marinate 120–50 g (4–5 oz) marbled sirloin or rib-eye beef in a mixture of soy, mirin and rice vinegar for at least an hour. Place in a colander and pour boiling water over the beef to sear the outside. Cut into very thin slices. Cut a whole medium-sized and very ripe nashi pear into thin julienned strips. Arrange the beef slices on a plate, cover with the julienned pear and drizzle with a mixture of tamari and sesame oil. Sprinkle with sesame seeds.

megrim & shiso cress usuzukuri sashimi
Prepare the basic recipe, replacing turbot with megrim and decorating with purple shiso cress in the ponzu sauce.

seared duck usuzukuri sashimi, nashi pear & tamari sesame oil dressing
Follow the seared beef usuzukuri recipe above, replacing beef with a duck breast.

variations

aburi salmon sashimi ceviche & truffle olive oil

see base recipe page 198

ebi tiger prawns sashimi, ceviche & truffle olive oil
Prepare the basic recipe, replacing salmon with 8–10 whole, large raw prawns. Aburi
blowtorch the prawns and cut into 2-cm (³/₄-in) pieces. Decorate with micro greens and a
little lime juice in your truffle olive oil.

scallop sashimi ceviche & truffle olive oil
Prepare the basic recipe, replacing salmon with 3–4 whole, large, dive-caught scallops. Aburi
blowtorch the scallops and cut into 2-cm (³/₄-in) pieces. Decorate as above.

white tuna sashimi ceviche, hijki & truffle olive oil
Prepare the basic recipe, replacing salmon with albacore tuna slices and decorate with
rehydrated hijiki seaweed and truffle olive oil.

lobster sashimi ceviche, coriander & truffle olive oil
Prepare the basic recipe, replacing salmon with 150 g (5 oz) raw lobster meat. Aburi
blowtorch the lobster meat, spoon the ceviche dressing over it. Finish by sprinkling with
coriander leaves, and drizzling small drops of truffle oil over all.

monkfish sashimi ceviche, coriander & truffle olive oil
Prepare the basic recipe, replacing salmon with 150 g (5 oz) raw monkfish tail. Aburi
blowtorch the monkfish tail, spoon the ceviche dressing over it. Finish as above.

variations

sesame-encrusted salmon sashimi
& spicy korean chilli dressing

see base recipe page 201

sesame-encrusted cod sashimi & jalapeño salsa
Prepare the basic recipe, replacing salmon with cod and the Korean chilli sauce with jalapeño salsa (page 54).

sesame-encrusted tofu & jalapeño salsa sashimi
Prepare the basic recipe, replacing salmon with 150 g (5 oz) (about half a standard pack size) firm tofu.

salt-and-pepper-encrusted salmon sashimi & apple–mustard sauce
Coat the salmon fillet with crushed black pepper and sea salt. Serve on the apple–mustard sauce (page 54).

salt-and-pepper-encrusted yellowtail sashimi & apple–mustard sauce
Prepare the basic recipe, replacing salmon with yellowtail fillet. Coat the yellowtail fillet with crushed black pepper and sea salt, and serve on the apple–mustard sauce (page 54).

salt-and-pink-pepper-encrusted beef sashimi, shallot & apple–mustard sauce
Prepare the basic recipe, replacing salmon with 150 g (5 oz) beef fillet. Coat the fillet with crushed pink pepper and sea salt, thinly slice the shallot and put in the centre. Serve on the apple–mustard sauce (page 54).

variations

squid sashimi & ikura salmon roe

see base recipe page 202

squid sashimi & mentaiko spicy pollock roe
Prepare the basic recipe, adding 2 teaspoons of pollock roe to the squid.

oyster, shallots & ponzu
Prepare the basic recipe, replacing squid with a large, shucked oyster. Add a teaspoon of ponzu sauce (page 39) and finely chopped shallot to the shell.

octopus ceviche & coriander
Prepare the basic recipe, replacing squid with raw octopus. Cut into slices rather than julienne strips and serve with ceviche sauce (page 43) and coriander leaves.

cuttlefish sashimi, ink & ikura salmon roe
Prepare the basic recipe, replacing squid with cuttlefish. Marinate the salmon roe with the ink of the cuttlefish, soy sauce and sake.

octopus sashimi, teriyaki & sesame

see base recipe page 205

cuttlefish sashimi & teriyaki
Prepare the basic recipe, replacing octopus with lightly boiled or
steamed cuttlefish.

prawn sashimi, soy sauce & sesame
Prepare the basic recipe, replacing octopus with prawns cooked as described on
page 225. Heat a mixture of soy sauce, mirin and sake. When cool, spoon it over
the prawns and sprinkle with sesame seeds. Place on top of julienned cucumber.

jellyfish sashimi, soy sauce & sesame
Prepare the basic recipe, replacing octopus with jellyfish. Normally you will
find them dried and sliced in an Asian grocery. They need to be soaked overnight
and then soaked again for 30 minutes in fresh water. Roll up the flesh and
slice it into thin julienne strips. Blanch the strips in boiling water then immerse
them in ice water. Heat a mixture of soy sauce, mirin and sake. When cool, mix
with a tablespoon of toasted sesame oil, and spoon it over the jellyfish and
sprinkle with sesame seeds. Place on top of the julienned cucumber.

variations

ankimo monkfish liver

see base recipe page 206

shirako cod milt
You will probably need to ask your fishmonger to obtain this for you. The
sperm sack is best served in a small bowl, topped with chopped spring onions,
wasabi and ponzu sauce (page 39).

ikura salmon roe
Marinate the salmon roe in a mixture of soy and sake for at least 4 hours. Pour
off the liquid, taking care not to break the eggs. Serve with soy and wasabi in a
hollowed-out piece of cucumber.

uni sea urchin
Serve the urchins just as they are in a piece of hollowed-out cucumber, with
soy and wasabi.

kazunoko herring roe
Herring roe has a fantastic crunchy texture. Serve on a bed of wakame
seaweed with soy and wasabi.

variations

korean-style sashimi & korean chilli sauce

see base recipe page 208

scallops, cockles, spinach & korean sashimi
Replace fish with 2 large scallops and 30 g (1 oz) cockles (out of shell weight).
Both the cockles and scallops can be served raw, but you can also steam them
if you prefer. Serve with wilted spinach tossed in a little sesame oil instead of
the micro greens.

tofu & spinach korean sashimi
Marinate a block of tofu in soy, mirin and rice vinegar. Cut into 2-cm
(³/₄-in) cubes and arrange over the rice, with wilted spinach tossed in
sesame oil, julienned carrot and julienned cucumber.

raw beef, pear & quail egg korean sashimi
This dish is inspired by Korea's famous dish of raw beef and pear. Chop
50 g (1³/₄ oz) marbled sirloin or rib-eye beef coarsely. Arrange julienned
cucumber, julienned carrot, and julienned pear over the rice. Top with the beef
and decorate with a raw quail egg.

temaki hand roll

Temaki really do have to be made just before you want to eat them, because if you leave the nori wrapped around the rice for even a few minutes, the crispness is lost and you are left having to tear into the temaki with all the pleasurable textures gone. Thus they are not ideal for picnics or parties, unless you want to get your friends around a table making their own.

yellowfin tuna, spring onion & wasabi mayonnaise temaki hand roll

see variations page 237

Temaki are usually served right at the end of a sushi dinner, when you are replete with sashimi and nigiri. The recipe here and its variations require super-fresh slices of raw fish, but unlike sashimi and nigiri cuts, they can be sliced from the shorter ends of the fish, so nothing is wasted. Temaki is mostly about getting the rolling technique right. After that, you can fill them with any number of things.

15 g (½ oz) yellowfin tuna fillet
½ sheet nori
30 g (1 oz) shari rice (page 28)
wasabi

2 tsp diagonally cut spring onion
white sesame seeds
1 tsp wasabi mayonnaise (page 50)

Cut the tuna into 5-cm (2-in) long slices. To make the temaki shape, be sure your left hand is dry and place the nori horizontally across your palm, holding it between your thumb and four fingers. Dip your right hand in vinegar water and pick up the rice. Spread it on the left-side of the nori. Dab a little wasabi paste over the rice to your liking. Once your rice is on the nori, dry your right hand and arrange the tuna slices and spring onion on the rice. Sprinkle with sesame seeds. Clean and dry your right hand again. The nori is now flat on your left palm. Pick up the bottom left corner of the nori with your right hand and pull it over the filling, aiming for the top of the nori sheet, and deftly tuck it under the filling. Gently turn with the left thumb to make an ice-cream-cone shape. Spoon a little wasabi mayonnaise over it to taste.

Makes 1 temaki

unagi faux eel kabayaki & cucumber temaki hand roll

see variations page 238

The sweet soy-basted faux eel is a particular favourite. It is well placed towards the end of a dinner when its denser texture and stronger tastes won't subvert the more delicate morsels – whitefish nigiri for example.

1 fillet of a dense white fish (We use lesser
    spotted dogfish, a kind of shark)
125 ml ($\frac{1}{2}$ fl. oz) cup soy sauce
3 tbsp sugar
3 tbsp mirin
3 tbsp sake

15 g ($\frac{1}{2}$ oz) cucumber, cut into thick,
    2-in lengths
1/2 sheet nori
30 g (1 oz) shari rice (page 28)
white sesame seeds

Eel populations are in serious danger of collapse. There are only two spawning grounds in the world, and both are dangerously overfished. Because eels can live until they are 80 and mate only once in their lives – just before they die – it is easy to see why they have become so vulnerable to overfishing. The wonder of this dish is that by cooking a good dense fish the same way as unagi is prepared in Japan, you get a really close alternative.

We use the lesser spotted dogfish, which is both abundant and virtually unused in the West. Get your fishmonger to fillet it and remove the skin, as it is tough and will dull your knife.

Wash under cold water. Combine the soy, sugar, mirin and sake until the sugar is dissolved. Place the fillet in the marinade and leave overnight in the refrigerator. Remove the fillet

from the marinade and place it in a steamer for 10 minutes. Then put under a grill, basting a little more of the marinade sauce on top, and grill until the surface is crisp. Reduce the remaining liquid and, when thickened, set aside to reserve for basting over the faux eel. Cut the grilled fillet into 5-cm (2-in) slices. Shape the temaki as described in the first recipe, page 221.

Makes 1 temaki, though there is enough fish fillet to make many more

ebi tiger prawn, avocado & wasabi mayonnaise temaki

see variations page 239

Cooked shellfish make excellent crunchy fillings in a temaki.

1 raw tiger prawns
salt
125 ml (4 fl. oz) mirin
125 ml (4 fl. oz) rice vinegar
½ sheet nori

30 g (1 oz) shari rice (page 28)
1 tbsp avocado, cut into thick 2-in lengths
white sesame seeds
1 tsp wasabi mayonnaise

You only use one prawn in each temaki but make as many hand rolls as you like. Skewer a whole, raw prawn from the tail to head just under the top shell. Drop the prawn into a saucepan of boiling, salted water and cook until the colour changes from translucent grey to pink, about 3 minutes. Remove from the water and cool, then remove the skewers. The prawn is cooked when it is bouncy to the touch. Pull off the head and peel the prawn carefully. Taking care to leave the tail intact, remove the shell and legs. Pat dry. Make an incision with a small sharp knife at the top of the inside of the prawn. Gently cut down to the tail so as to butterfly-open the prawn, taking care not to cut through the flesh. Wash under running water to remove any grey innards clinging under the spine.

Combine the mirin and vinegar and marinate the prawns for 30 minutes. Remove and pat dry. After that you can use immediately, or easily store them in the freezer. Roll the temaki as described on page 221, and sprinkle with sesame seeds. Spoon a little wasabi mayonnaise over it to taste.

Makes 1 temaki

crisp salmon skin teriyaki
& spring onion temaki hand roll

see variations page 240

Teriyaki flavours are good to finish a sushi dinner with. Robust in flavour, they should come after the more delicate raw fish in sashimi and nigiri.

45 g (¾ oz) of salmon skin, try to leave a thin
    layer of salmon flesh under the skin
salt
1 tsp teriyaki sauce (page 36)

½ sheet nori
30 g (1 oz) shari rice (page 28)
2 tsp finely chopped spring onion

Take the salmon skin pieces, cover lightly with sea salt on both sides, and place under a grill until it is crispy brown and the skin starts to bubble and darken. Set aside to cool. It should now feel nearly brittle.

Cut the salmon skin into long lengths and brush with the teriyaki sauce. Make the temaki with the spring onion as described on page 221.

Makes 1 temaki

negitoro tuna, mayonnaise & spring onion temaki hand roll

see variations page 241

The taste of toro tuna was probably what first led me to open a sushi bar; the creaminess of the flesh of the belly of the bluefin tuna is quite divine. Bluefin tuna fetch extraordinary prices these days, the record recently being about £470,000 for one fish! The astonishing decline of bluefin stocks has been well documented. I simply can't bring myself to profit at the expense of such a beautiful and noble creature, so toro came off our menus in 1998. And I can honestly say that I've not missed it – now I much prefer to see these incredible animals on television as they circumnavigate the globe with their intelligence and awesome grace.

20 g (³/₄ oz) yellowfin tuna fillet, the end of the cut is fine
1 tsp wasabi mayonnaise (page 50)
¹/₂ sheet nori
30 g (1 oz) shari rice (page 28)
2 tsp finely chopped spring onion

Makes one temaki, but make up as much of the tuna mix as you like.

Mince your tuna very finely, using a large knife and chopping it until it becomes soft and mushy. Mix with the wasabi mayonnaise.

Make the temaki with the spring onion as described on page 221.

Makes 1 temaki

natto fermented soybean & spring onion temaki hand roll

see variations page 242

This section features a selection of classic Japanese vegetarian ingredients, which are often some of the hardest for non-Japanese people to get their head around. Natto fermented soybean has become a personal favourite of mine, but it took me a long time, and a flight on a Japanese airline with little to eat but dried natto snacks, to finally acquire the taste. Once someone in Japan realises that you are quite familiar with their culture, their next question is always 'So, can you eat natto?' Not to be outdone in the culinary stakes, I persevered, and now I love the stuff.

1 tbsp natto fermented soybean	30 g (1 oz) shari rice (page 28)
½ sheet nori	2 tsp finely chopped spring onion

Fermenting soybeans to become natto is a step too far for the scope of this book, and natto is commonly purchased in tubes or small plastic packets that can be frozen. It doesn't last long once opened, so the frozen option is a good one.

Make the temaki with the natto and spring onion as described on page 221. Use a teaspoon or chopsticks to spread the natto because you will soon appreciate its peculiar gooey and sticky traits!

Makes 1 temaki

pumpkin & burdock tempura temaki hand roll

see variations page 243

Tempura, long associated with Japan, was probably a legacy of the sixteenth-century Portuguese missionaries who would eat only fish on Fridays and often deep-fried it. The word itself is thought to be a Japanification of templo, the Portuguese word for temple. Non-traditional in Japan, tempura sushi rolls are a favourite in the West.

1 burdock root
½ pumpkin, cut into medium juliennes about
    5-cm (2-in) long
1 tsp rice vinegar

batter for 4 rolls
250 g (8 oz) plain flour, plus a little extra
    for coating

1 large egg
375 ml (12 oz) ice water and ice cubes

vegetable oil, for deep-frying
2 nori sheets
150 g (5 oz) shari rice (page 28)
white sesame seeds
chilli mayonnaise (page 50)

Burdock comes in a long muddy root. Scrub (rather than peel) the outside well to remove the dirt. Lightly scrape off the skin with a knife (burdock is deemed to be a very healthy root, and much of the nutrient and flavour content lies just under the skin, so best preserve it). Cut into medium julienned strips about 5-cm (2-in) long. Once cut, place them in a bowl of cold water with a teaspoon of rice vinegar in it to avoid discolouration.

Now make the tempura batter. The secret is not to beat the batter too vigorously, so mix the flour, egg and ice water with chopsticks and leave lumps of flour unblended. You can also add ice cubes if you like.

Heat the vegetable oil in a small deep saucepan to 175°C/Gas Mark 4 (350°F). Alternatively, test the temperature by flicking in a drop of batter – it should sink and then rise; if it just sinks it is too cool, and if it rises straight away it is too hot. Coat the burdock and pumpkin juliennes in a little flour, remove the excess, then dip into the batter. Immerse in the hot oil for about 3 minutes, or until the batter has turned golden. Remove the vegetables with a stainless mesh spoon and drain on a wire rack or kitchen towels.

Make the temaki with the tempura vegetables as described on page 221. Sprinkle with sesame seeds and serve with chilli mayonnaise.
Makes 4 temaki

katsu chicken, cucumber & tonkatsu mayonnaise temaki hand roll

see variations page 244

Breaded and deep-fried dishes make popular lunchtime meals, and tonkatsu, breaded and deep-fried pork, is nearly always served along with shredded white cabbage and tonkatsu sauce, a spicy (but not hot) thick brown sauce. In the West we use chicken, which feels better suited to sushi, though neither would be found in traditional sushi.

vegetable oil, for frying
1 egg
100 g (3½ oz) fillet chicken breast or thigh
salt and pepper to season
2 tbsp plain flour
5 tbsp breadcrumbs

2 nori sheets
150 g (5 oz) shari rice (page 28)
60 g (2 oz) julienned cucumber
tonkatsu mayonnaise (page 50)
shiso cress, to garnish

Heat the oil in a deep saucepan to 175°C/ Gas Mark 4 (350°F) degrees. Beat the egg. Sprinkle the chicken with salt and pepper. Line up the beaten egg, a plate of flour and a plate of breadcrumbs side by side. Coat the chicken with the flour, shake off the excess, then dip in the beaten egg, then into the breadcrumbs and put straight into the hot oil. Cook until crisp and golden brown on the outside, remove with a long slotted spoon and drain on kitchen towels. Cut the chicken into four diagonal slices. Make the temaki roll with a slice of katsu chicken and cucumber using the rolling technique described on page 221. Spoon some tonkatsu mayonnaise and a sprinkle of shiso cress over it to serve.
Makes 4 temaki

tuna salad with sweetcorn temaki

see variations page 245

Sushi tends to favour raw fish, but there are a few things that work well cooked in temaki, and tinned tuna is easy and versatile to use, and a relatively common stuffing in everyday, homemade sushi.

150 g (5 oz) tinned tuna in water
4 tsp finely chopped onion
30 g (1 oz) sweetcorn

210 g (7½ oz) shari rice (page 28)
3 sheets nori
6 tsp wasabi mayonnaise (page 50)

Drain the tinned tuna. Combine the tuna, onion, sweetcorn and wasabi mayonnaise together. Make the temaki as described in the recipe on page 221.

Makes 6 temaki

variations

yellowfin tuna, spring onion &
wasabi mayonnaise temaki hand roll

see base recipe page 221

salmon & avocado temaki
Prepare the basic recipe, replacing tuna with salmon and avocado slices, a sprinkle of sesame seed and wasabi mayonnaise.

bream, shiso cress, cucumber & yuzukosho temaki
Prepare the basic recipe, replacing tuna with slices of bream and cucumber, shiso cress and a dab of yuzukosho paste.

bass, red radish, cucumber & jalapeño salsa temaki
Prepare the basic recipe, replacing tuna with slices of bass and cucumber, finely sliced red radish and a teaspoon of jalapeño salsa (page 54).

hamachi yellowtail, spring onion & tobiko flying fish roe temaki
Prepare the basic recipe, adding a teaspoon of flying fish roe.

mackerel, asparagus, shiso cress & yuzu mayonnaise temaki
Prepare the basic recipe, replacing tuna with slices of mackerel, blanched asparagus, 1 teaspoon mustard, and shiso cress and a teaspoon of yuzu mayonnaise (page 34).

hamachi yellowtail, red radish, red pepper & jalapeño salsa temaki
Prepare the basic recipe, adding red radish, red pepper and jalapeño salsa (page 54).

variations

unagi faux eel kabayaki & cucumber temaki hand roll

see base recipe page 222

duck leg, cucumber, chilli & chives temaki
Prepare the basic recipe, replacing faux eel with meat from a duck leg. Roll with finely chopped chilli and chives.

beef fillet, red onion & mizuna temaki
Prepare the basic recipe, replacing faux eel with 15 g (½ oz) marbled sirloin or rib-eye beef, omitting the steaming stage. Thinly slice the red onions and roll with mizuna.

enoki mushrooms & mizuna temaki
Prepare the basic recipe, replacing faux eel with enoki mushrooms, which don't need marinating and won't take long under the grill. Roll with mizuna leaves and a sprinkle of sesame seeds.

unagi faux eel kabayaki dogfish, green beans & avocado temaki
Prepare the basic recipe, adding blanched green beans and a slice of avocado.

variations

ebi tiger prawn, avocado &
wasabi mayonnaise temaki

see base recipe page 225

prawn, mizuna, pine nuts & yuzu mayonnaise temaki
Prepare the basic recipe. Roll with mizuna leaves, yuzu mayonnaise and pine nuts.

prawn, ikura salmon roe & lettuce temaki
Prepare the basic recipe, and roll with lettuce leaves. Top with salmon roe.

squid, cucumber & ume plum temaki
Prepare the basic recipe, replacing prawns with julienned strips of raw squid as prepared on page 17. Add julienne slices of cucumber and a dash of ume plum puree.

crab & avocado temaki
Prepare the basic recipe, replacing prawns with 15 g (½ oz) mixed fresh brown and white crabmeat. Add some slices of avocado and sprinkle with sesame seeds.

crab, spring onion & yuzu mayonnaise temaki
Prepare the basic recipe, replacing prawns with 25g (¾ oz) mixed fresh brown and white crabmeat. Add some chopped spring onion and a teaspoon of yuzu mayonnaise (page 50).

lobster, avocado, tobiko flying fish roe & wasabi mayonnaise temaki
Prepare the basic recipe, replacing prawns with lobster as prepared on page 62. Add slices of avocado, flying fish roe and wasabi mayonnaise (page 50).

crisp salmon skin teriyaki & spring onion temaki hand roll

see base recipe page 226

chicken skin teriyaki, cucumber & mizuna temaki
Prepare the basic recipe, replacing salmon skin with chicken skin. Wrap the temaki, using slices of cucumber and mizuna leaves.

beef teriyaki, green beans & watercress temaki
Crisp a few slices of beef under a grill, basting with teriyaki sauce. Blanch the green beans and wrap them with sprigs of watercress.

squid teriyaki & asparagus temaki
Grill a few slices of squid, basting with teriyaki sauce. Wrap with blanched asparagus.

teriyaki quail, fig & lettuce temaki
Grill a few slices of quail meat, basting with teriyaki sauce. Wrap with fig slices and lettuce.

teriyaki shiitake mushroom, burdock & sesame temaki
Rehydrate the shiitake by soaking in water for 20 minutes. Prepare and cool burdock and mushrooms as described on page 252. Spoon over a little teriyaki sauce.

shishito pepper & red pepper teriyaki temaki
Halve and deseed a whole shishito and cut two 5-cm (2-in) lengths of red pepper. Grill, basting with teriyaki sauce. Cut to size and wrap. Sprinkle with shiso cress or mustard and cress.

negitoro tuna, mayonnaise & spring onion temaki hand roll

see base recipe page 228

chopped salmon & cucumber temaki

Prepare the basic recipe, replacing tuna with salmon, and wrap the temaki with julienned cucumber. Squeeze over a little lime juice to serve.

chopped scallop & shiso leaf temaki

Prepare the basic recipe, replacing tuna with ½ a whole, large scallop, chopped. Mix with some shredded shiso leaf and minced shallots. Combine this with yuzu mayonnaise and add a dash of lime juice.

chopped snapper in ceviche dressing, mizuna & shiso cress temaki

Prepare the basic recipe, replacing tuna with chopped snapper (any firm bream or flatfish will do). Mix with a teaspoon of ceviche sauce (page 43). Wrap the temaki with the ceviche snapper, adding mizuna and shiso cress.

chopped yellowtail & spring onion temaki

Prepare the basic recipe, replacing tuna with yellowtail ('hamachi' or 'buri' in Japanese).

chopped bass & shiso leaf temaki

Prepare the basic recipe, replacing tuna with bass. Mix with some shredded shiso leaf and minced shallots. Combine this with yuzu mayonnaise and add a dash of lime juice.

variations

natto fermented soybean & spring onion temaki hand roll

see base recipe page 230

umeboshi pickled plum & cucumber temaki
Replace natto with umeboshi. Umeboshi can be found in Japanese groceries, or in health food shops, with the best quality brand in Europe being Clearspring. To make the wrap, use the puree form, or mash the whole plum yourself, adding plenty of cucumber to cool down the tartness.

natto fermented soybean & okra temaki
Prepare the basic recipe, adding a sprinkling of chopped okra.

umeboshi pickled plum, daikon radish & green bean temaki
Make a temaki using blanched green beans, julienned strips of daikon radish, and a daub of ume plum.

umeboshi pickled plum & shiso temaki
Shred some shiso leaves, add julienned cucumber and daub on some ume plum. Ume and shiso are a classic combination.

simmered bamboo & cucumber temaki
Prepare bamboo as described on page 247. Make the wrap with julienned cucumber and sprinkle with sesame seeds.

pumpkin & burdock tempura temaki hand roll

see base recipe page 232

tempura softshell crab, avocado & chilli mayonnaise temaki
Prepare the basic recipe, replacing burdock with softshell crab cut into quarters.
Wrap using a teaspoon of chilli mayonnaise (page 50) and slices of avocado.
Scatter flying fish roe over the temaki.

tempura prawn, cos lettuce, avocado & wasabi mayonnaise temaki
Prepare the basic recipe, replacing burdock with prawns, leaving the tails on for
a decorative effect. Wrap using a teaspoon of wasabi mayonnaise (page 50),
slices of avocado and lettuce leaves. Scatter with torn shiso cress.

tempura squid, mizuna, chilli, sea salt & lime temaki
Prepare the basic recipe, replacing burdock with squid. Wrap with mizuna leaves,
chopped red chilli and sprinkle with a little sea salt and lime zest.

tempura avocado & smoked paprika mayonnaise temaki
Prepare the basic recipe, replacing burdock with 1 quartered avocado. Wrap
using a teaspoon of smoked paprika mayonnaise (page 50).

tempura courgette flower stuffed with burrata temaki
Stuff a courgette flower with burrata cheese and carefully seal the flower before
coating it in batter and frying. Wrap, spooning on a teaspoon of honey to taste.

variations

katsu chicken, cucumber & tonkatsu mayonnaise temaki hand roll

see base recipe page 234

tonkatsu pork & white cabbage temaki
Prepare the basic recipe, replacing chicken with fried fillet of pork. Wrap with shredded white cabbage and a spoonful of tonkatsu mayonnaise.

prawn katsu, mizuna & wasabi mayonnaise temaki
Prepare the basic recipe, replacing chicken with four tiger prawns in fried breadcrumbs, katsu style, and wrap with mizuna leaves and wasabi mayonnaise (page 50).

prawn katsu, avocado & chilli mayonnaise temaki
Prepare the basic recipe, replacing chicken with prawns in fried breadcrumbs, katsu style and wrap with a slice of avocado and sweet chilli mayonnaise (page 50).

shirako cod milt katsu, lettuce heart & jalapeño salsa temaki
Prepare the basic recipe, replacing chicken with prawns in fried breadcrumbs, katsu style, and 90 g (3 oz) shirako, the sperm sac of cod from a Japanese supermarket. Wrap the shirako katsu with contrasting crunchy lettuce hearts and a spoonful of jalapeño salsa (page 54).

salmon katsu, avocado, spring onion & yuzu mayonnaise temaki
Prepare the basic recipe, replacing the chicken with salmon in fried breadcrumbs, katsu style, and wrap with a slice of avocado. Add chopped spring onion and a spoonful of yuzu mayonnaise.

variations

tuna salad with sweetcorn temaki

see base recipe page 236

tuna salad with red radish, watercress & onion temaki
Prepare the basic recipe, adding onion red radish and wasabi mayonnaise.

kakuni poached salmon, watercress & wasabi mayonnaise temaki
Prepare the basic recipe, replacing tuna with salmon poached as described on page 256.
Mix with the mayonnaise and wrap with watercress.

kakuni poached salmon, rocket & wasabi mayonnaise temaki
Prepare the basic recipe, replacing tuna with salmon poached as described on page 256.
Mix with the wasabi mayonnaise and wrap with rocket leaves.

kakuni tuna, soy & ginger temaki
Prepare the basic recipe, replacing tinned tuna with tuna poached as described on page 256.
Mix with the wasabi mayonnaise and wrap with rocket leaves and oroshi ginger.

kakuni bass, cucumber & katsuo boshi bonito temaki
Prepare the basic recipe, replacing tuna with bass poached as described on page 256.
Mix with wasabi mayonnaise and a sprinkle of katsuo boshi. Wrap with julienned cucumber.

chirashi, onigiri & pressed sushi

Whilst sushi is generally considered the purview of experts, chirashi, inari and onigiri are all types of sushi that are commonly made at home. They generally require less knife technique, and rice moulding skills are not as important. Their versatility means that you can often use whatever leftover fish or vegetables you may have on hand.

chirashi of shiitake mushroom, lotus root & bamboo

see variations page 269

Chirashi means 'scattered sushi', and usually refers to raw fish. Here vegetables are used instead.

3 shiitake mushrooms
125 ml (4 fl. oz) soy sauce
3 tbsp sake
3 tbsp apple juice or 3 tbsp sugar
1/2 renkon lotus root, cut into very thin slices and then into quarters, reserving 2 whole slices for decoration
1/2 takenoko bamboo shoot (from a tin or vacuum pack), cut into 5-cm (2-in) lengths
1 carrot, cut into 2-cm (3/4-in) diagonal chunks

5 runner beans cut into diagonal 3.75-cm (1 1/2-in) lengths, or green beans
1/4 pouch of abura-age fried tofu
brown rice
4 tsp tamago omelette (page 189, not strictly necessary but very traditional)
1/4 nori sheet, shredded
200 g (7 oz) shari rice (page 28) or genmai brown rice (page 28)

Place the shiitake in a cup of hot water and leave to rehydrate for about 20 minutes. Remove the shiitake and combine the remaining water with the soy, sake and apple juice in a small saucepan. Put the shiitake, lotus root, bamboo and carrot into the saucepan and bring to the boil. Simmer for about 4 minutes, until the liquid has nearly evaporated. Steam or blanch the green beans, plunge into cold water, and add to the cooled other vegetables. Cut the abura-age into 2-cm (3/4-in) long, fine strips. Finely shred the tamago sweet omelette and the nori seaweed. Place the warm rice in a bowl. Arrange the vegetables on top, scatter the green beans, abura-age and omelette on top, and decorate with the lotus root and shredded nori.

Makes 1 bowl

classic chirashi scattered fish

see variations page 270

This is the classic Tokyo-style scattered fish on a bowl of rice. There are no set rules as to which fish to choose here, so pick your favourites.

1 tsp dried wakame seaweed
200 g (7 oz) shari rice (page 28)
4 tsp shredded daikon
1 shiso leaf
3 slices of salmon, cut as sashimi
3 slices of snapper or bream, cut as sashimi
3 slices of marinated mackerel, cut as sashimi
3 slices of tuna
2 boiled tiger prawns

2 slices of boiled octopus
2 large strips of tamago omelette (page 189)
lemon slices
1 tsp ikura salmon roe
wasabi
1 tsp pickled ginger
julienned cucumber
1 tsp shiso cress or mustard and cress

Rehydrate the wakame seaweed in a little water for a few minutes, drain well. Fill a bowl with sushi rice. Classic white rice works best, but you can use genmai brown rice if you prefer. Arrange the grated daikon at the far edge of the bowl alongside the wakame. Place the shiso leaf on top of the daikon.

Arrange the slices of fish and tomago as you like over the rice, taking into consideration the balance of colour. Add slices of lemon alongside the whitefish (snapper or bream) to add contrast. Decorate with ikura salmon roe.

Place a daub of wasabi to one side. Garnish with a piece of pickled ginger, julienned cucumber and shiso cress.

Makes 1 bowl

seared beef chirashi with red wine & wasabi jus

see variations page 271

This is a totally unconventional yet delicious chirashi, and I feel traditionalists around the world recoiling in horror! Too delicious not to include here, it proves that it's worth trying something new.

4 tsp daikon oroshi grated white radish
½ chilli
¼ red onion
ice water
3 tbsp wasabi powder
2 tbsp water
4 tbsp soy sauce
3 tbsp mirin

125 g (4 oz) beef fillet
sea salt and pepper
2 tsp butter for frying
3 tbsp red wine
white truffle oil
1 tsp sansho peppercorns (or pink peppercorns)
200 g (7 oz) shari rice (page 189)
2 tsp spring onion, finely chopped

Mix the grated daikon with finely chopped chilli. Finely slice the red onion and place in a bowl of ice water for 10 minutes. Drain and set aside. Mix the wasabi powder with the water until dissolved, and blend with the soy sauce. Add the mirin to the soy–wasabi liquid. Rub salt and pepper into the beef fillet. Heat butter in a saucepan and sear the fillet, about 1 minute on each side. Keeping the beef juices in the pan, add the soy, wasabi and mirin mix and use a high heat to reduce. Add the red wine and reduce further. Last, add a splash of white truffle oil and sansho peppercorns. Slice the beef fillet to make a sashimi-style appearance. Fill a bowl two-thirds full with shari rice and arrange the beef slices on top. Pour on a little of the red wine wasabi jus and garnish with the sliced red onion, spring onion and chilli oroshi daikon. Serve remainder of the red wine wasabi jus in a separate jug.

Makes 1 bowl (the sauce will be enough for 4 portions)

inari sushi stuffed with kinpira burdock & carrot

see variations page 272

Inari is made from deep-fried tofu, or abura-age, which is cut into thin slices, press-drained and deep-fried again.

½ burdock root
1 tsp rice vinegar and a bowl of ice water
1 carrot
2 tsp white sesame seeds
½ tbsp mirin
2 tbsp soy sauce

3 tbsp dashi (page 44)
1 red chilli
1 tbsp toasted sesame oil
2½ tbsp shari rice (page 28)
2 inari pouches, washed (purchased as they are
    from a Japanese grocery)

Burdock will come in a long muddy root. Scrub (rather than peel) the outside well to remove the dirt and lightly scrape off the skin with a knife. Burdock is a very healthy root and much of the nutrient and flavour content lies just under the skin, so try to preserve it. Cut into thin julienned strips about 2.5-cm (1-in) long. Once cut, place the strips into a bowl of cold water with a teaspoon of rice vinegar to prevent them from discolouring. After peeling the carrot, cut it into similar julienned strips. Roast the sesame in a dry pan. Combine the mirin, soy and dashi in a bowl. Finely chop the chilli. Strain and dry the burdock. In a frying pan heat the sesame oil and add the burdock and carrot. Sauté over a medium heat until slightly softened. Then add the mirin, soy and dashi and simmer gently with the lid off for 5–10 minutes until the liquid is mostly absorbed. Take it off the heat and stir in the chilli and toasted sesame seeds. Mix this 'kinpira' mixture with the shari rice. Stuff the prepared inari with the shari rice and kinpira mixture. Fold the inari into a small neat parcel.
Makes 3 inari

inari sushi stuffed with edamame soybean & jamón

see variations page 273

The little stuffed tofu pouches also lend themselves to less traditional combinations. Here we take inspiration from the classic Spanish tapas dish habas con jamón, beans with ham.

10 edamame beans, boiled
20 g (¾ oz) serrano or iberico ham
2½ tbsp shari rice (page 28)

2 inari pouches, washed (purchased as they are from a Japanese grocery)
black pepper

Edamame beans can usually be found in the freezer section of a grocery shop, and come ready shelled, like peas. Boil these beans briefly, so that they remain firm.

Chop the ham into small pieces and mix into the rice with the boiled edamame. Season with black pepper. Stuff the prepared inari with the rice, ham and edamame mixture. Fold the inari into a small, neat parcel to serve.

Makes 3 inari

onigiri rice balls & oven-poached salmon

see variations page 274

Rice is of extraordinary importance in Japanese culture, and no more so as when used in the humble rice ball onigiri, which is considered a meal in itself.

110 g (3½ oz) salmon fillet
250 ml (8 fl. oz) soy
125 ml (4 fl. oz) rice vinegar
125 ml (4 fl. oz) mirin

300 g (9 oz) boiled white short-grain rice
2 nori sheets
sea salt

A plastic onigiri mould helps if you have one, but it isn't necessary.

Place the salmon in a small ovenproof dish. Combine the soy, vinegar and mirin and pour over the salmon. Poach in an oven preheated to 175°C/Gas Mark 4 (350°F) for about 10–15 minutes, depending on the thickness of your fillet. When cool, shred into small pieces. Stir in the cooked rice with a pinch of salt. Mix the rice and the shredded salmon together. Take a large handful (100 g/3 oz) of the salmon-rice in your hand and press until it doesn't fall apart. Make a spherical shape first, then gently press between your palms to create a more triangular shape. That will slightly flatten the ball. Cut a sheet of nori into a long length of the same width as your onigiri. Wrap the onigiri as shown in the picture on page 274. If you live near a Japanese grocery, you may find this style of elaborate wrapping there. It's designed especially so the nori won't get soggy!

Makes 4 onigiri

picnic-wrapped tuna salad onigiri

see variations page 275

A more homely style of onigiri is to partially wrap it in nori, making it yet more portable – this style is often chosen for picnics. From a Japanese viewpoint, there is something very comforting about this style of onigiri; it is just as your mum might have made for your school lunch box.

150 g (5 oz) tinned tuna in water
4 tsp finely chopped onion
400 g (12 oz) boiled white short-grain rice

1 nori sheet
white sesame seeds

A plastic onigiri mould helps if you have one, but it isn't necessary.

Drain the tinned tuna and combine with the chopped onion.

Take a large handful (100 g/3 oz) of rice in your hand, and press until it doesn't fall apart. Make a spherical shape and then make a small indentation in one side. Spoon into the hollow of a teaspoon of tuna–onion mix. Press the rice together to conceal it. Once you have the spherical shape again, gently press between your palms to create a more triangular shape, slightly flattening the ball.

Cut a sheet of nori into 4 pieces. Wrap a piece of it around the centre of the onigiri as shown in the picture on page 275. Sprinkle with sesame seeds.

Makes 4 onigiri

yaki-grilled rice balls onigiri

see variations page 276

The grilled rice ball is another popular version of the humble onigiri, often found in local pub-style izakayas, and usually served with pickles.

400 g (12 oz) boiled short-grain rice
4 tsp soy sauce
pickles

Make the onigiri rice ball shape as described in the recipe on page 256.

Grill on each side for about 2 minutes. Brush with a teaspoon of soy sauce and place under the grill again just to toast off. Be wary of adding too much soy, as this will break up the rice.

Serve with a bowl of miso soup, oshinko pickles or cucumber pickles.

Makes 4 onigiri

classic japanese vegetables in onigiri rice balls

see variations page 277

Furthering the notion of the onigiri being the perfect snack food for its portability and ease of making, using traditional Japanese vegetable ingredients also helps prolong its shelf life on picnics or packed lunches.

3 tbsp hijiki seaweed
soy sauce
400 g (12 oz) boiled white short-grain rice

1 nori sheet
black sesame seeds

Hijiki is a type of dark brown seaweed that looks like small twigs. It is high in calcium and contains plenty of fibre. Hijiki seaweed can be purchased at a Japanese grocery in its dry form, so you will need to rehydrate it in water for 30 minutes or so. Once softened, drain and mix with a dash of soy sauce.

Make the onigiri rice ball shape as described in the base recipe (page 256), placing the hijiki in the small hollow.

Cut a sheet of nori into 4 pieces. Wrap a piece around the centre of the onigiri as shown in the picture opposite. Sprinkle with black sesame seeds.

Makes 4 onigiri

cabbage parcels, tamago, rice & peas

see variations page 278

This is a delightful little addition to any picnic, and it's not as hard as it looks!

4 large savoy cabbage leaves
ice water
40 g (1½ oz) tamago omelette (page 189)
mitsuba leaves or chives

80 g (2¾ oz) shari rice (page 28)
1 tbsp peas, blanched
toasted black sesame seeds
cocktail sticks

Cut out the hard stem at the base of the cabbage. Blanch the cabbage leaves in a large saucepan of boiling water for a minute. Remove and immediately plunge into ice water, preventing the leaves from losing their colour.

Dice the tamago omelette. Chop the mitsuba leaves and mix with the shari rice, peas, tamago and sesame seed.

Place one cabbage leaf on a chopping board and spoon on top a quarter of the rice mixture. Fold over the bottom and top of the cabbage leaf and then the sides, making a neat parcel. Secure it with a cocktail stick.

Makes 4 cabbage parcels

oshi zushi pressed sushi ham & cheese

see variations page 279

Pressed sushi is the oldest form of sushi and was first used as a means of preserving fish by packing it tightly in a box of fermenting rice. In the earliest forms of sushi, only the preserved fish was eaten and the rice was actually discarded.

80 g (2¾ oz) cured ham, sliced very thinly
20 g (¾ oz) iceberg lettuce leaves, uncut
80 g (2¾ oz) Gruyère (or any hard cheese of
   your choice), cut into very thin slices

Japanese mustard
125 g (4 oz) shari rice (page 28)

Traditionally, this is made using a wooden mould, but if you don't have one, then use an oblong cake loaf tin with sides as straight as possible. The traditional size of a mould is 15 x 7.5 cm (6 x 3 in). If you are using a loaf tin, line it with clingfilm. If you are using a wooden mould, soak it in water to prevent the rice from sticking. Arrange the ham in layers at the bottom of the container. Add a layer of iceberg leaves. Top with a layer of Gruyère and smear a little mustard over the cheese (as desired). Add the shari rice to the mould or loaf tin, and use your fingers to pack down the rice. Put the lid on the mould and press it down to compact the rice. Remove the sides of the mould by pressing on the lid, then take the lid off and carefully turn the mould over and eject the block onto a chopping board, with the ham side now facing up. To make it more decorative, you can arrange the ingredients with diagonal slices of hard cheese placed first, as pictured. Wrap in clingfilm and store in a cool place (ideally not as cool as a refrigerator) for up to 5 hours. When ready to use, dip a sharp knife in water and cut the block into 6 equal pieces.
Makes 6 pieces

oshi zushi pressed sushi with atsu-age deep-fried tofu

see variations page 280

When I first went to Japan, the slightly grubby station kiosks were always full of forsaken-looking boxes of pressed mackerel sushi. Nowadays, oshi zushi is little seen other than the infrequent packed lunch for school, though the nostalgia lingers at railway bento-box kiosks, where the traditional version of vinegared mackerel is always something to pick up for a train trip back to your hometown.

100 g (3½ oz) atsu-age dried and fried tofu
4 tsp pickled cucumber (page 49)
½ avocado

wasabi
125 g (4 oz) shari rice (page 28)
1 nori sheet cut to size of container

Atsu-age or abura-age (a smaller version of it) can be found in Japanese groceries and should be rinsed in hot water to remove the excess oil. Cut into 3-mm (⅓-in) thick slices and line the bottom of a mould with it, making sure there are no gaps. Cut the pickled cucumber into long, thin slices and lay over the abura-age. Roughly chop the avocado and layer on top of the cucumber. Smear with wasabi to taste.

Fill the rice half way and pack down, then place the cut piece of nori on top of the rice. Add the remainder of the rice and pack down. Continue making the oshi zushi as described in the previous recipe (page 265).

Makes 6 pieces

halloumi cheese & greek salad rice bowl with yuzu vinaigrette

see variations page 281

A quick, healthy, and easy light lunch; essentially a rice salad with endless possibilities to use your favourite vegetables and cheese.

soy sauce, for glazing
30 g (1 oz) diced halloumi cheese
30 g (1 oz) diced avocado
30 g (1 oz) diced red pepper
30 g (1 oz) diced cherry tomato
30 g (1 oz) diced cucumber
½ tsp mizuna

½ oz black olives, pitted and halved
400 g (12 oz) shari rice (page 28)
sea salt & black pepper
sesame seeds
nori, to garnish
2 tsp yuzu vinaigrette (page 52)

Brush a little soy sauce over the halloumi cheese and grill on each side for a minute or so until golden on each side. Gently mix all the diced vegetables and mizuna together with the halloumi and arrange on top of a bowl of warm shari rice, reserving a few black olives for decoration. Sprinkle with salt and pepper, garnish with the olives and strips of cut nori and serve with a yuzu vinaigrette.

It is also nice to serve this dish with the rice mixed gently in with the chopped vegetables, creating a shari rice salad. Brown rice is of course also lovely to use here.

Makes 1 portion

variations

chirashi of shiitake mushroom, lotus root & bamboo

see base recipe page 247

tamago omelette, gammon & shishito peppers chirashi
Prepare the basic recipe, replacing vegetables with 2 shredded shishito peppers and 30 g (1 oz) tamago omelette. Replace tofu with 40 g (1½ oz) gammon, cut into 1-cm (⅓-in) cubes. Sprinkle with nori to serve.

ume plum & shiso chirashi
Prepare the basic recipe, replacing vegetables with 3–4 whole umeboshi plums, omitting marinade and tofu. Tear 2 shiso leaves and mix with 1 tablespoon ume plum puree. Sprinkle over plums, with sesame seeds and nori on top.

edamame soybean & jamón chirashi
Prepare the basic recipe, replacing vegetables with 30 g (1 oz) steamed soybeans and tofu with 45 g (1½ oz) jamón, cut into cubes. Scatter on top with soybeans, tamago and nori.

kinpira burdock & carrot chirashi
Omit vegetables, marinade, omelette and tofu. Prepare burdock root and carrot as described on page 252. Top with sesame seeds, chopped spring onions and shredded nori.

tororo mountain yam potato and tuna chirashi
Omit vegetables, marinade, omelette and tofu. Grate 50 g (1¾ oz) Japanese mountain yam, or nagaimo, chop marinated cubes of tuna (page 58) and serve sprinkled with spring onion.

variations

classic chirashi scattered fish

see base recipe page 248

aji no tataki chopped horse mackerel & spring onion chirashi
Prepare the basic recipe, replacing fish with 80 g (2¾ oz) horse mackerel as prepared on page 94. Mix with 30 g (1 oz) chopped spring onion and 2 teaspoons ponzu sauce and decorate with wasabi and long pieces of chives.

negitoro 'belly of tuna' and spring onion chirashi
Prepare the basic recipe, replacing fish with tuna as prepared on page 222. Arrange on top of 30 g (1 oz) chopped spring onion and 15 g (½ oz) shredded iceberg lettuce. Decorate with wasabi and long pieces of chives.

scallop & ikura salmon roe chirashi
Prepare the basic recipe, replacing fish with 2 large scallops as prepared on page 110 and cut into cubes. Julienne about 30 g (1 oz) cucumber. Place the scallops over the cucumber, top with 2 teaspoons salmon roe, and decorate with shiso cress.

unagi 'faux eel' kabayaki chirashi
Prepare the basic receipe, replacing fish with faux eel as prepared on page 222. Top with shichimi pepper and some pickles on the side, as you like.

salmon ju
Prepare the basic receipe, replacing fish with slices of salmon sashimi. Serve covering a bed of rice topped with a blob of wasabi and a teaspoon of salmon roe.

seared beef chirashi with red wine & wasabi jus

see base recipe page 251

seared duck with umeshu plum wine & wasabi jus chirashi
Prepare the basic recipe, replacing beef with duck, searing skin-side down first, omitting butter when frying. Replace mirin and red wine with 6 tablespoons of plum wine.

seared chicken with sake & wasabi jus chirashi
Prepare the basic recipe, replacing beef with chicken breast, searing skin-side down first, but cook the chicken longer so as to cook through the centre. Replace mirin and red wine with 6 tablespoons of sake.

seared quail with red wine & wasabi jus chirashi
Prepare the basic recipe, replacing beef with quail breast, searing skin-side down first and frying for a slightly shorter time.

seared venison with umeshu plum wine & wasabi jus chirashi
Prepare the basic recipe, replacing beef with venison. Replace mirin and red wine with 6 tablespoons of plum wine.

inari sushi stuffed with kinpira burdock & carrot

see base recipe page 252

spinach & sesame inari
Omit burdock and carrot. Blanch a few spinach leaves for 20 seconds and drain. Toast
1 teaspoon white sesame seeds in a dry heavy-bottomed saucepan and then grind them in a
mortar. Prepare a mixture of soy sauce with your choice of apple juice, sugar or mirin. Add
the ground sesame seeds and mix well. Add spinach, mix with the rice and stuff the inari.

tamago omelette & Japanese mushrooms inari
Prepare the basic recipe, replacing burdock and carrot with a selection of shiitake, enoki or
nameko mushrooms. Mix with shreds of omelette before stuffing.

ginko nut & shiso inari
Prepare the basic recipe, replacing burdock and carrot with 10 whole, ready-prepared ginko
nuts from a Japanese supermarket, crushed. Mix with 2 torn shiso leaves before stuffing.

renkon lotus root & nira garlic shoots inari
Prepare the basic recipe, replacing burdock and carrot with equal quantities of renkon and
garlic shoots, prepared in the kinpira style.

pickled ginger, kanpyo calabash gourd strips & carrot inari
Prepare the basic recipe, replacing burdock and carrot with calabash strips and carrot
prepared in the kinpira style. Mix with a little chopped pickled ginger before stuffing.

variations

inari sushi stuffed with edamame soybean & jamón

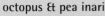

see base recipe page 255

octopus & pea inari
Prepare the basic recipe, replacing jamón with octopus as prepared on page 74 and replacing edamame with boiled green peas.

tataki beef inari
Prepare the basic recipe, replacing jamón with beef as prepared on page 198, chopped into small pieces. Omit edamame.

halloumi & sunblush tomato inari
Prepare the basic recipe, replacing jamón with 30 g (1 oz) halloumi cheese, toasted and cut into chunks. Replace edamame with 2 tablespoons chopped sunblush tomato.

simmered pumpkin & walnut inari
Prepare the basic recipe, replacing jamón with nimono-style simmered pumpkin as described on page 73, chopped into small chunks. Replace edamame with walnuts, toasted in a dry pan and then crushed.

mentaiko chilli pollock roe & lime inari
Prepare the basic recipe, replacing jamón and edamame with 30 g (1 oz) mentaiko chilli pollock roe (available from Japanese grocery stores). Mix into shari rice with a little lime zest.

variations

onigiri rice balls & oven-poached salmon

see base recipe page 256

tuna kakuni with soy ginger onigiri
Prepare the basic recipe, replacing salmon with tuna, poached with one teaspoon of grated ginger.

poached tuna with shichimi onigiri
Prepare the basic recipe, replacing salmon with tuna, poached with a sprinkle of shichimi pepper.

poached salmon with yuzukosho onigiri
Prepare the basic recipe. When the poached salmon is cool, shred it and mix in ½ teaspoon of yuzu kosho paste.

furikake onigiri
Prepare the basic recipe, replacing salt with furikake (a rice seasoning available at most Japanese grocery stores, containing sesame seeds, wasabi powder, and other spices such as sansho pepper). Omit salmon.

picnic-wrapped tuna salad onigiri

see base recipe page 257

katsuo boshi bonito flakes onigiri
Prepare the basic recipe, omitting tuna. Fill the hollow with some bonito flakes and a tiny dash of soy.

sunblush tomato, spring onion & mozzarella onigiri
Prepare the basic recipe, omitting tuna. Finely chop 4 sunblush tomatoes, 4 teaspoons spring onion and 25 g (¾ oz) mozzarella and spoon into the hollow.

tuna salad & sweetcorn onigiri
Prepare the basic recipe, adding 60 g (2 oz) sweetcorn to the tuna before filling the hollow.

tuna salad & jalepeño onigiri
Prepare the basic recipe, adding 30 g (1 oz) of finely chopped jalepeño to the tuna before filling the hollow.

variations

yaki-grilled rice balls onigiri

see base recipe page 259

genmai brown rice yaki onigiri
Prepare the basic recipe, replacing rice with genmai brown rice (page 47).

teriyaki-glazed yaki onigiri
Prepare the basic recipe, replacing soy sauce with teriyaki sauce (page 36).

bacon & mozzarella yaki onigiri
Prepare the basic recipe. Grill one side first, then top the second side of each onigiri with a very thin slice of mozzarella and ½ a strip of bacon. Grill until bacon is cooked through.

cheese & green pepper yaki onigiri
Prepare the basic recipe. Grill on one side first, then top the second side with a hard cheese such as Gruyère. Sprinkle chopped green pepper on top and grill until the cheese has melted.

oshinko pickle yaki onigiri
Prepare the basic recipe, placing a round slice of oshinko pickled daikon radish on top, just before the soy sauce is brushed on.

bamboo shoot yaki onigiri
Prepare the basic recipe, topping one side with a slice of boiled bamboo just before the soy sauce is brushed on.

variations

classic japanese vegetables in onigiri rice balls

see base recipe page 260

natto fermented soybean & spring onion onigiri
Prepare the basic recipe, replacing seaweed with 70 g (2½ oz) chopped spring onion mixed
with 70 g (2½ oz) natto.

pickled cucumber onigiri
Prepare the basic recipe, replacing seaweed with chopped pickled cucumber as prepared in
on page 49.

ume plum & shiso onigiri
Prepare the basic recipe, replacing seaweed with 4 whole umeboshi plums mixed with
2 chopped shiso leaves.

moromiso & spring onion onigiri
Prepare the basic recipe, replacing seaweed with 70 g (2½ oz) moromiso paste mixed with
70 g (2½ oz) chopped spring onion.

variations

cabbage parcels, tamago, rice & peas

see base recipe page 262

tamago omelette, pea & gomoku brown rice cabbage parcel
Prepare the basic recipe, replacing rice with 5-grain rice (page 47).

edamame & gammon cabbage parcel
Prepare the basic recipe, replacing the peas with boiled edamame and replacing the tamago with small pieces of gammon. Season with Japanese mustard.

halloumi cheese & sunblush tomato cabbage parcel
Prepare the basic recipe, replacing the tamago with 50 g (1½ oz) halloumi, toasted and cut into small chunks. Omit peas and mix rice with 4 chopped sunblush tomatoes.

edamame & chorizo cabbage parcel
Prepare the basic recipe, replacing the peas with boiled edamame and replacing the tamago with small pieces of chorizo. Season with smoked paprika mayonnaise (page 50).

halloumi cheese & olive cabbage parcel
Prepare the basic recipe, replacing the tamago with 50 g (1½ oz) halloumi, toasted and cut into small chunks. Omit peas and mix rice with 6 chopped green or black olives.

oshi zushi pressed sushi gammon & cheese

see base recipe page 265

bamboo shoot & pine nut pressed sushi

Prepare the basic recipe, replacing gammon and cheese with 90 g (3 oz) bamboo shoots and 4 teaspoons pine nuts. Using tinned or vacuum-packed bamboo, simmer as on page 73. Cut into thin slices and sprinkle with pine nuts before pressing down the rice.

tataki seared beef & shiso cress pressed sushi

Prepare the basic recipe, replacing gammon and cheese with beef and cress. Sprinkle shiso cress on the bottom of the mould. Prepare the tataki beef as described on page 198, place the beef on top of the shiso cress and smear with a bit of wasabi or Japanese mustard.

avocado & smoked paprika mayonnaise pressed sushi

Prepare the basic recipe, omitting gammon and cheese. Line the mould with ½ large avocado, cut into slices, and smear with a little smoked paprika mayonnaise (page 50).

yuba soy milk skin & wasabi pressed sushi

Prepare the basic recipe, replacing gammon and cheese with 4 slices yuba (which can be purchased pre-sliced in a specialist Japanese grocery) and smear with a little wasabi.

variations

oshi zushi pressed sushi with atsu-age deep-fried tofu

see base recipe page 266

vinegared mackerel pressed sushi
Prepare the basic recipe, replacing atsu-age with vingegared mackerel as prepared on page 61, and lay the slices across the base of the mould. Smear with a little wasabi.

prawns pressed sushi
Prepare the basic recipe, replacing atsu-age with prawns as prepared on page 225. Line the mould with the prawns, top-side down, and add wasabi as desired.

faux eel unagi pressed sushi
Prepare the basic recipe, replacing atsu-age with faux unagi eel as prepared on page 222. Line the mould with the faux eel, basting with a little of the sauce.

lemon sole, shiso pressed sushi
Prepare the basic recipe, replacing atsu-age with a fillet of sole, cut to size, and line the mould. Place the shiso leaf on the sole. The pressed result when turned out of the mould shows the green of the shiso shining through the translucence of the sole flesh.

tamago omelette pressed sushi
Prepare the basic recipe, replacing atsu-age with a 0.5-cm (1/3-in) thick piece of omelette placed at the bottom of the mould.

halloumi cheese & greek salad rice bowl with yuzu vinaigrette

see base recipe page 268

tamago omelette, gammon & shishito peppers rice bowl
Prepare the basic recipe, omitting cheese and olives. Cut 60 g (2 oz) organic gammon into 1.75-cm (½-in) cubes, scatter on top of the rice with shreds of omelette. Salt and gently grill 2 shishito peppers, deeseeded and sliced. Arrange on the rice and sprinkle with shreds of nori.

ume plum & shiso rice bowl
This is a classic combination, and as the ume plums are so tart, you won't need to cover the whole surface of the bowl. Tear some leaves of shiso and mix with the puree of 4 whole umeboshi plums, sprinkle sesame seeds and nori on top.

edamame, soybean & jamon rice bowl
Prepare the basic recipe, omitting cheese and olives. Cut 60 g (2 oz) Spanish-style ham into cubes, steam 2 tablespoons soybeans, and scatter on top with shreds of tamago omelette and nori.

index

Aburi hamachi yellowtail 70, 86

aburi salmon sashimi ceviche & truffle olive oil 198, 214

aji horse mackerel in rice vinegar nigiri 81

aji no tataki horse mackerel & spring salmon onion chirashi 270

aji no tataki horse mackerel gunkan 94, 113

aji no tataki horse mackerel sashimi 212

akagai red clam nigiri 82

ama ebi sweet prawn 82, 113, 211

ama ebi sweet prawn nigiri 82

ama ebi sweet prawn sashimi, jalapeño salsa, daikon & lime olive oil 211

ama ebi sweet prawn tataki & avocado gunkan 113

anchovy in rice vinegar nigiri 81

ankimo monkfish liver 84, 206, 218

ankimo monkfish liver nigiri 84

apple-mustard sauce 54, 215

asparagus 120, 126, 137, 141, 162, 237, 240

asparagus & bacon teriyaki 126, 138

asparagus, green bean & green pepper gunkan 120

asparagus hosomaki 137

avocado 83, 87, 97, 113, 114, 116, 137, 141, 145, 149, 154, 156, 169, 177, 182, 183, 186, 225, 237, 239, 243, 244, 266, 268, 279

avocado, jalapeño & coriander salsa nigiri 83

avocado & sesame hosomaki 137

avocado & smoked paprika mayo futomaki 178

avocado & smoked paprika mayo nigiri 87

avocado & smoked paprika mayo pressed sushi 279

avocado & ume plum uramaki 157, 179

Bacon 126, 276

bacon & mozzarella yaki onigiri 276

baked foie gras gunkan 117

baked scallop & ponzu butter gunkan 117

bamboo hosomaki 136

bamboo shoot & pine nut pressed sushi 279

bamboo shoot gunkan 120

bamboo shoots (takenoko) 120, 242, 247, 279

bamboo shoot yaki onigiri 276

bass 79, 89, 143, 166, 208, 237, 241, 245

bass, red radish, cucumber & jalapeño salsa temaki 237

bass, spring onion & ginger nigiri 79

bass & yuzukosho tempura hosomaki 143

beans
  edamame 139, 255, 269
  green 120, 143, 150, 176, 183, 242, 247

beef 77, 84, 117, 138, 150, 162, 183, 213, 215, 219, 238, 240, 251, 273, 279

beef, fig & green bean uramaki 183

beef fillet, red onion & mizuna temaki 238

beef teriyaki, green beans & watercress temaki 240

bonito flakes 44, 275

bream 142, 172, 237, 241, 248

bream & shiso hosomaki 142

bream, shiso cress, cucumber & yuzukosho temaki 237

bream, ume plum & cucumber futomaki 172

broccoli, purple sprouting 179

brown rice & bamboo hosomaki 128, 139

brown rice, ham, peas & carrot 139

brown rice with kinpira burdock & carrot 139

brown rice, red rice, ume plum, shiso & edamame 139

brown rice, sesame, adzuki, red rice & millet 139

burdock 141, 178, 179, 232-3, 240
  kinpira 139, 175, 252, 269

burdock & carrot uramaki 179

Cabbage parcels, tamago, rice & peas 262, 278

calabash 49, 137, 180, 272

california crab, flying fish roe & avocado uramaki 149, 174

capelin roe see masago capelin roe

caviar 77, 112, 174, 177, 187, 206, 209

caviar gunkan 112

ceviche sauce 43, 54

cheese & green pepper yaki onigiri 276

chicken 119, 183, 234, 240, 271
  bones 36

chicken with ginger, sake, sesame & soy gunkan 119

chicken skin teriyaki, cucumber & mizuna temaki 240

chicken, yuzokosho & spinach uramaki 183

chilli 43, 49, 88, 115, 119, 150, 164, 172, 177, 181, 183, 238, 243, 251, 252

chilli mayo 50, 98

Chinese cabbage & chilli pickles 49

chirashi, onigiri & pressed sushi 246-81

chirashi of shiitake mushroom, lotus root & bamboo 247, 269

chopped bass & shiso leaf temaki 241

chopped salmon & cucumber temaki 241

chopped scallop & shiso leaf temaki 241

chopped snapper in ceviche dressing, mizuna & shiso cress temaki 241

chopped yellowtail & spring onion temaki 241

chorizo 90, 181

chorizo & smoked paprika mayo nigiri 90

classic chirashi scattered fish

248, 270

classic japanese vegetables in onigiri rice balls 260, 277

cockles 219

cod 141, 184, 215

cod, mizuna & katsuo boshi uramaki 184

coriander-chilli salsa 83

crab & avocado gunkan 97, 114

crab & avocado temaki 239

crab claw tempura, chives & yuzu mayo gunkan 115

crabmeat 89, 97, 114, 149, 154, 239, 243

crabmeat & spring onion gunkan 114

crab, spring onion & yuzu mayo temaki 239

crabstick & tobiko 142

creamy spicy white miso dip 53

crisp salmon skin teriyaki & spring onion temaki hand roll 226, 240

crispy salmon skin futomaki 146, 173

cucumber and daikon tsuma 46

cuttlefish 116, 121, 216, 217

cuttlefish & shiso gunkan 121

cuttlefish ceviche & cucumber gunkan 116

cuttlefish ink 216

cuttlefish sashimi & teriyaki 217

cuttlefish sashimi, ink & ikura salmon roe 216

Daikon white radish 27, 46, 76, 114, 117, 136, 154, 172, 175, 179, 190, 193, 194, 198, 202, 208, 209, 242, 248

oroshi 85, 86, 88, 89, 90,

135, 193, 196, 198, 251

daikon in sake pickles 49

dashi 43, 52, 73, 78, 106, 109, 120, 128, 189, 209, 252

dashi stock 44, 55

dogfish, lesser spotted 222-3

dover sole & caviar 209

dragon roll prawn, salmon & avocado uramaki 169, 186

duck 84, 102, 118, 175, 181, 213, 238, 271

duck with dengaku white miso gunkan 118

duck leg, cucumber, chilli & chives temaki 238

Ebi tiger prawn, avocado & wasabi mayo temaki 225, 239

ebi tiger prawn sashimi, ceviche & truffle olive oil 214

edamame & chorizo cabbage parcel 278

edamame & ham cabbage parcel 278

edamame soy bean & jamón chirashi 269

edamame, soy bean & jamón rice bowl 281

eel, faux see faux eel

enoki mushroom gunkan 120

enoki mushroom hosomaki 137

enoki mushrooms & mizuna temaki 238

Faux eel 142, 173, 182, 186, 222-3, 238, 270, 280

faux eel, cucumber & avocado dragon roll 186

faux eel, salmon & avocado dragon roll 186

faux eel unagi pressed sushi 280

fish, choosing and filleting 16-18

flounder, spring onion & ginger yubiki nigiri 85

flying fish roe see tobiko

foie gras 66, 84, 117, 138, 182

foie gras & asparagus hosomaki 138

foie gras & pomegranate nigiri 66, 84

foie gras poached nashi pear, umeshu plum wine & cucumber uramaki 182

fried asparagus hosomaki 141

fried avocado hosomaki 141

fried burdock hosomaki 141

fried cod hosomaki 141

fried courgette hosomaki 141

fried prawn hosomaki 133, 141

fried sweet potato hosomaki 141

furikake onigiri 274

futomaki 22-3, 144-87

Gammon, pineapple & cress uramaki 183

genmai brown rice 47

genmai brown rice yaki onigiri 276

ginger, gari pickled 32, 49

ginko nut & shiso inari 272

goat's cheese, chive & walnut hosomaki 130, 140

gochujang miso stew 48

gomoku (5-grain) rice 47

gorgonzola & celery hosomaki

140

green bean tempura hosomaki 143

grey mullet in soy sauce, mirin & sake nigiri 80

grilled shishito pepper nigiri 73, 87

Gruyère 140, 156, 265, 276

Gruyère & sunblush tomato hosomaki 140

gunkan battleship sushi 92-121

gyoza dumplings, mizuna & daikon futomaki 179

Haddock, smoked 184

halloumi & sunblush tomato inari 273

halloumi cheese & greek salad rice bowl with yuzu vinaigrette 268, 281

halloumi, grilled shishito & pancetta uramaki 182

halloumi cheese & olive cabbage parcel 278

halloumi cheese & sunblush tomato cabbage parcel 278

ham 139, 209, 265, 269, 278, 281

iberico 255

serrano 255

hamachi yellowtail 70, 79, 83, 84, 113, 135, 193, 215, 237, 241

hamachi yellowtail & chives nigiri 79

hamachi yellowtail, jalapeño & coriander salsa nigiri 83

hamachi yellowtail, red radish, red pepper & jalapeño salsa temaki 237 hamachi yellowtail sashimi, herb ceviche sauce & ponzu olive oil 193, 211

hamachi yellowtail, spring onion & tobiko temaki 237

hamachi yellowtail tataki & shiso gunkan 113

herring 81, 212

herring in rice vinegar nigiri 81

herring roe 112

hijiki seaweed 46, 214, 260

hijiki seaweed & daikon tsuma 46

honey & soy quail with fig & cucumber futomaki 161, 181

hon-mirin 36, 55

horse mackerel 79, 81, 94, 212, 270

horse mackerel, spring onion & ginger nigiri 79

hosomaki 122-43

Ikura salmon roe 202, 218, 248, 270

ikura salmon roe classic gunkan 93, 112

inari 246
  pouches 252, 255

inari sushi stuffed with edamame soybean & jamón 255, 273

inari sushi stuffed with kinpira burdock & carrot 252, 272

inari tofu nigiri 87

Jalapeño 43, 85, 185, 193, 275

jalapeño salsa 54

jamón 269

jellyfish sashimi, soy sauce & sesame 217

John Dory, ikura salmon roe & chives 210

Kabayaki faux eel 173, 182

kabayaki faux eel & cucumber 142

kabayaki faux eel & cucumber futomaki 173

kabayaki faux eel, cucumber & avocado uramaki 182

kakuni bass, cucumber & katsuo boshi bonito temaki 245

kakuni poached salmon, watercress & wasabi mayo temaki 245

kakuni tuna, soy & ginger temaki 245

kanpyo calabash gourd pickles 49, 137

kanpyo pickled calabash gourd hosomaki 137

kappamaki hosomaki 137

katsu chicken, cucumber & tonkatsu mayo temaki hand roll 234, 244

katsu deep-fried salmon & fennel futomaki 173

katsuo boshi 166, 245,

katsuo boshi bonito flakes onigiri 275

kazunoko herring roe 218

kazunoko herring roe gunkan 112

kinpira burdock & carrot chirashi 269

knives, Japanese 14-15

konbu kelp 39, 44, 47, 55

korean-style sashimi & korean chilli sauce 208, 219

Langoustine & avocado gunkan 114

lemon sole 80, 119, 172, 210, 213

lemon sole, ginger oroshi & leeks 210

lemon sole with ginger, sake, sesame & soy gunkan 119

lemon sole, sea salt & lime yubiki nigiri 85

lemon sole & shiso futomaki 172

lemon sole, shiso pressed sushi 280

lemon sole in soy sauce, mirin & sake nigiri 80

lemon sole usuzukuri sashimi 213

lobster 62, 114, 115, 174, 176, 177, 214, 239

lobster & avocado uramaki 174

lobster & chive gunkan 114

lobster & yuzu mayo futomaki wrap 176

lobster, avocado, tobiko & wasabi mayo temaki 239

lobster, avocado, wasabi mayo & caviar futomaki wrap 177

lobster sashimi ceviche, coriander & truffle olive oil 214

lobster tail & yuzu mayo nigiri 62, 82

lobster tempura & lemon gunkan 115

lotus root & shiitake mushroom gunkan 120

lotus root (renkon) 48, 120, 247

Mackerel 61, 194, 237, 248, 280

mackerel, asparagus, shiso cress & yuzu mayo temaki 237

mackerel, spring onion & ginger nigiri 61, 81

maki rolling technique
  futomaki 22-3
  uromaki 24-5

marinated beef hosomaki 138

marinated sashimi of mackerel, spring onion & oroshi ginger 194, 212

marinated tofu nigiri, ginger & spring onion 87

marinated tuna nigiri 58, 80

masago capelin roe 112, 170, 187

masago capelin roe gunkan 112

mayonnaise (mayo) 34, 50, 98

megrim & shiso cress usuzukuri sashimi 213

mentaiko chilli pollock roe 152, 273

mentaiko chilli pollock roe & lime inari 273

mentaiko pollock roe & creamy wasabi sauce gunkan 118

mentaiko pollock roe gunkan 112

miso dengaku 105

miso soup 30, 48

mitsuba leaves 48, 66, 174, 209, 262

mitsuba trefoil leaf 143

mixed seaweed tsuma 46

mizuna leaves 152, 166, 177, 179, 184, 238, 239, 240, 241, 243, 268

monkfish 115, 119, 184, 214

monkfish with coriander, sake,

sesame & soy gunkan 119
monkfish liver 206
monkfish sashimi ceviche,
    coriander & truffle olive
    oil 214
monkfish tempura, lime &
    sansho pepper gunkan 115
moromiso & spring onion
    onigiri 277
moromiso paste 277
mountain yam (nagaimo)
    212, 269
mozzarella 138, 182, 275, 276
mozzarella & smoked salmon
    uramaki 182
mozzarella & sunblush tomato
    hosomaki 140
mugi miso paste 30

Natto (fermented soybean)
    136, 230, 277
natto & okra temaki 242
natto & spring onion hosomaki
    136
natto & spring onion onigiri
    277
natto & spring onion temaki
    hand roll 230, 242
negitoro 'belly of tuna' and
    spring onion chirashi 270
negitoro tuna belly & spring
    onion futomaki 172
negitoro tuna, mayo & spring
    onion temaki hand roll
    228, 241
nigiri sushi 20-1, 56-91
nimono daikon 156
nimono shiitake mushroom
    & smoked paprika mayo
    nigiri 87

Octopus 74, 118, 176, 205, 216,
    248, 273
octopus & dengaku white miso
    gunkan 118
octopus & nori nigiri 88
octopus & pea inari 273
octopus ceviche & coriander
    216
octopus ceviche & red pepper
    gunkan 100, 116
octopus, chilli, oroshi daikon &
    lime nigiri 88
octopus, cucumber & spring
    onion futomaki wrap 176
octopus nigiri 74, 88
octopus sashimi, teriyaki &
    sesame 205, 217
okra & sesame hosomaki 137
okra 120, 136, 137
    nimono-style 174
okra gunkan 120
onigiri 246
onigiri rice balls & oven-
    poached salmon 256, 274
oshinko pickle 125, 187, 276
oshinko pickled daikon
    hosomaki 125, 137
oshinko pickle yaki onigiri 276
oshi zushi (pressed sushi) 9
oshi zushi with atsu-age deep-
    fried tofu 266, 280
oshi zushi ham & cheese
    265, 279
oyster & dengaku white miso
    gunkan 118
oyster & yuzu mayo futomaki
    wrap 177
oysters 115, 118, 177, 216
oyster, shallots & ponzu 216
oyster tempura & chilli gunkan

115

Pancetta 138, 182
pancetta, mozzarella & chive
    hosomaki 138
panfried beef & teriyaki
    mustard sauce uramaki
    150, 175
panfried beef, asparagus,
    burdock, chilli & spring
    onion uramaki 175
panfried beef with teriyaki &
    yuzukosho oroshi gunkan
    117
panfried chorizo & green &
    yellow pepper futomaki 181
panfried duck, cucumber,
    spring onion & carrot with
    hoisin sauce uramaki 175
panfried duck, green beans,
    carrot, chilli & spring onion
    uramaki 175
panfried duck, green beans,
    daikon radish, sesame seeds
    & spring onion uramaki 175
panfried duck, pomegranate,
    soy sauce & honey gunkan
    102, 117
panfried tuna, chives & korean
    chilli sauce gunkan 117
panfried tuna, green beans,
    carrot, chilli & spring onion
    uramaki 175
panfried tuna with wasabi
    mayo uramaki 175
pear, nashi 182, 213
pickled cucumber onigiri 277
pickled ginger, avocado & red
    pepper uramaki 179
pickled ginger, kanpyo calabash

gourd strips & carrot inari
    272
pickles 32, 49
plaice 76, 113, 116
plaice ceviche & spring onion
    gunkan 116
plaice tataki, ume plum &
    chive gunkan 113
poached bass with katsuo
    boshi & yuzukosho uramaki
    166, 184
poached monkfish, cucumber &
    prosciutto uramaki 184
poached salmon, asparagus &
    wasabi mayo futomaki 173
poached salmon with
    yuzukosho onigiri 274
poached tuna with shichimi
    onigiri 274
pollock roe 112, 118, 216
pomegranate seeds 66, 90, 102
ponzu butter 52
ponzu sauce 39, 52
pork 244
prawn 114, 186, 217, 243, 280
    brown 209
    ebi tiger 133, 214
    jumbo 133
    tiger 80, 82, 98, 119, 169,
        174, 176, 177, 225,
        244, 248
prawn & avocado dragon
    roll 186
prawn, ikura salmon roe &
    lettuce temaki 239
prawn katsu, mizuna & wasabi
    mayo temaki 244
prawn, mizuna, pine nuts &
    yuzu mayo temaki 239
prawn pressed sushi 280

prawn sashimi, soy sauce &
  sesame 217
prawns, avocado & chilli mayo
  futomaki wrap 177
prawns with chilli, sake, sesame
  & soy sauce gunkan 119
prawn tempura gunkan 97, 115
prawn & yuzu zest gunkan 114
prosciutto 184
pumpkin & burdock tempura
  temaki hand roll 232-3, 243
pumpkin-burdock tempura &
  sesame futomaki 178
purple sprouting broccoli &
  sesame uramaki 179

Quail 90, 161, 181, 240, 271
quail eggs 219

Radish, red 168, 173, 237, 245
raw beef, pear & quail egg
  korean sashimi 219
raw lobster, oroshi daikon &
  ponzu gunkan 114
razor clam with yuzu, sake,
  sesame & soy gunkan 119
red miso, burdock & carrot 48
red miso, shiitake mushroom &
  nira garlic shoots 48
red mullet 85, 190-1
red snapper 69, 190-1, 210
red snapper & ume plum 210
renkon lotus root & nira garlic
  shoots inari 272
rice, shari sushi 28-9, 47
Roquefort & endive hosomaki
  140

Saikyo miso 40, 53
saikyo miso & lotus root 48

saikyo miso & snapper 48
saintly vegetarian stained glass
  window futomaki 187
sake & konbu shari rice 47
salmon 57, 64, 89, 113, 116,
  142, 145, 169, 173, 174,
  187, 190-1, 198, 201, 208,
  211, 237, 241, 244, 245, 248,
  256, 274
  skin 146, 226
  smoked 83, 182, 187
salmon & avocado futomaki
  145, 172
salmon & avocado temaki 237
salmon & caviar stained glass
  window futomaki 187
salmon hosomaki 142
salmon, jalapeño salsa &
  avocado gunkan 116
salmon – ju 270
salmon katsu, avocado, spring
  onion & yuzu mayo temaki
  244
salmon nigiri 57, 79
  tea-smoked 64, 83
salmon roe 93, 112, 210,
  239, 270
  see also ikura salmon roe
salmon sashimi 270
salmon sashimi herb ceviche,
  daikon & ponzu olive oil 211
salmon tataki & avocado
  gunkan 113
salt-and-pepper-encrusted
  salmon sashimi & apple-
  mustard sauce 215
salt-and-pink pepper-
  encrusted beef sashimi,
  shallot & apple-mustard
  sauce 215

samphire with butter teriyaki
  gunkan 120
sardines 81, 212
sardines in rice vinegar
  nigiri 81
sashimi 188-219
scallop & avocado uramaki 174
scallop & ikura salmon roe
  chirashi 270
scallop & mitsuba tempura
  hosomaki 143
scallop & shiso futomaki
  wrap 176
scallop & shiso nigiri 82
scallop, ceviche & shiso gunkan
  121
scallop sashimi ceviche &
  truffle olive oil 214
scallop sashimi, jalapeño salsa,
  daikon & lime olive oil 211
scallops 82, 89, 110, 115, 117,
  143, 174, 211, 214, 219,
  241, 270
scallops, cockles, spinach &
  korean sashimi 219
scallop with shiso gunkan
  110, 121
scallop tempura & shiso
  gunkan 115
scorched bass, daikon oroshi &
  yuzukosho nigiri 89
scorched king crab & wasabi
  mayo nigiri 89
scorched plaice nigiri 76, 89
scorched scallop & shiso
  nigiri 89
scorched tuna, sea salt & black
  pepper nigiri 89
seared beef & pink peppercorn
  nigiri 84

seared beef chirashi with red
  wine & wasabi jus 251, 271
seared beef uramaki 162, 182
seared beef usuzukuri sashimi,
  nashi pear & tamari sesame
  oil dressing 213
seared chicken with sake &
  wasabi jus chirashi 271
seared duck & chives nigiri 84
seared duck & grapefruit
  uramaki 164, 183
seared duck, spring onion &
  red chilli futomaki 181
seared duck with umeshu
  plum wine & wasabi jus
  chirashi 271
seared duck usuzukuri sashimi,
  nashi pear & tamari sesame
  oil dressing 213
seared hamachi yellowtail &
  wasabi nigiri 84
seared quail & chestnut
  futomaki 181
seared quail with red wine &
  wasabi jus chirashi 271
seared tuna, korean chilli sauce
  & spring onion nigiri 84
seared venison with umeshu
  plum wine 271
sea urchin 86, 105, 112, 118,
  218
sea urchin uni roe & sea salt
  aburi nigiri 86
seaweed tsuma, mixed 46
sesame dressing 53
sesame-encrusted cod sashimi
  & jalapeño salsa 215
sesame-encrusted salmon
  sashimi & spicy korean chilli
  dressing 201, 215

sesame-encrusted tofu &
    jalapeño salsa sashimi 215
shari rice 28-9, 47
shari vinegar 80
shichimi pepper 54, 83, 89,
    172, 184, 270
shiitake mushroom gunkan
    109, 120
shirako cod 118
shirako cod milt 218, 244
shirako cod milt & spring onion
    gunkan 118
shirako cod milt katsu, lettuce
    heart & jalapeño salsa
    temaki 244
shishito peppers 73, 156,
    240, 269
shishito pepper & red pepper
    teriyaki temaki 240
shishito pepper stuffed with
    gorgonzola & honey 178
shiso & cucumber uramaki 179
shiso & ume plum nigiri 87
shiso juice 43
shiso leaf 46
simmered bamboo & cucumber
    temaki 242
simmered pumpkin & walnut
    inari 273
smoked haddock, mizuna &
    prosciutto uramaki 184
smoked paprika mayo 50
snapper 241, 248
soboro stained glass window
    futomaki 187
softshell crab daikon wrap
    154, 177
sole, yuzukosho & orosho
    daikon aburi nigiri 86
soy marinade 58, 87, 88, 212

sweet 212, 222
spicy tuna & shichimi 7-spice
    pepper futomaki 172
spinach & sesame inari 272
squid 106, 115, 142, 152, 174,
    177, 202, 239, 240, 243
squid & mizuna wrapped in
    cucumber 152, 176
squid & shiso nigiri 88
squid, chilli & lime nigiri 88
squid, cucumber & ume plum
    temaki 239
squid with ginger, sake, soy &
    sesame gunkan 106, 119
squid, mizuna, chilli, sea salt &
    lime futomaki wrap 177
squid sashimi & ikura salmon
    roe 202, 216
squid sashimi & mentaiko spicy
    pollock roe 216
squid tempura & chilli gunkan
    115
squid teriyaki & asparagus
    temaki 240
squid, ume plum & cucumber
    hosomaki 142
squid, ume plum & spring
    onion nigiri 88
squid with ume plum, shiso &
    caviar uramaki 174
stained glass window futomaki
    170-1, 187
sunblush tomato, spring onion
    & mozzarella onigiri 275
sushi etiquette 10-12
sweet chilli mayo 50

Tamago & chestnut 209
tamago & green pepper 209
tamago with adzuki bean

sweet nigiri 91
tamago with brown prawns 209
tamago with ham 209
tamago, mitsuba & halloumi
    209
tamago omelette 170-1, 247,
    248, 262, 269, 280, 281
tamago omelette & Japanese
    mushrooms inari 272
tamago omelette, ham &
    shishito peppers chirashi 269
tamago omelette, ham &
    shishito peppers rice bowl
    281
tamago omelette nigiri 78, 91
tamago omelette, pea &
    gomoku rice cabbage
    parcel 278
tamago omelette pressed
    sushi 280
tamago sweet omelette sashimi
    189, 209
tamago with shiitake
    mushroom 209
tamari 213
tamari wafu dressing 52
tataki beef & caviar nigiri
    77, 90
tataki beef inari 273
tataki duck & pomegranate
    nigiri 90
tataki quail & spring onion
    nigiri 90
tataki seared beef & shiso cress
    pressed sushi 279
tataki tuna & korean chilli
    mayo aburi nigiri 86
tea-smoked salmon nigiri
    64, 83
tea-smoked salmon, soy,

mirin, kimchee & shichimi
    7-spice chilli pepper garnish
    nigiri 83
tekkamaki - tuna hosomaki
    134, 142
temaki hand roll 220-45
tempura avocado & smoked
    paprika mayo temaki 243
tempura courgette flower
    stuffed with burrata temaki
    243
tempura dipping sauce 55
tempura shishito pepper
    futomaki 156, 178
tempura softshell crab,
    avocado & chilli mayo
    temaki 243
tempura squid, mizuna, chilli,
    sea salt & lime temaki 243
teriyaki with korean chilli
    sauce 51
teriyaki quail, fig & lettuce
    temaki 240
teriyaki sauce 36, 51
teriyaki shiitake mushroom,
    burdock & sesame temaki
    240
tiger prawn & avocado uramaki
    174
tiger prawn & okra uramaki
    174
tiger prawn & yuba with
    sweet chilli mayo futomaki
    wrap 176
tiger prawn in gari ginger juice
    nigiri 80
tiger prawn, green beans
    & smoked paprika mayo
    futomaki wrap 176
tiger prawn nigiri 82

tiger prawn, salmon, cream
cheese & avocado uramaki
174
toasted tofu futomaki 158
tobiko (flying fish roe) 142,
145, 146, 149, 152, 154, 170,
177, 184, 237, 239
tofu 30, 48, 52, 86, 87, 158,
215, 219, 247
abura-age 247
atsu-age 266
inari 87, 252
tofu & spinach korean sashimi
219
tofu dengaku 86
tofu & saikyo miso sauce aburi
nigiri 86
tofu sesame salad dressing 52
tonkatsu mayo 50
tonkatsu pork & white cabbage
temaki 244
tonkatsu sauce 50
tororo (mountain yam) &
marinated tuna sashimi 212
tororo & tuna chirashi 269
tsuma – sashimi decoration 27,
46, 190, 209
tuna 58, 84, 86, 89, 117, 134,
173, 184, 186, 190-1, 208,
211, 212, 245, 248, 269,
270, 274
albacore 160, 214
canned 168, 236, 257
yellowfin 79, 113, 168, 172,
221, 228, 237
tuna & avocado dragon roll
186
tuna, cucumber & spicy flying
fish roe uramaki 184
tuna kakuni with soy ginger

onigiri 274
tuna nigiri 79
tuna salad & black olive
futomaki 185
tuna salad & jalapeño onigiri
275
tuna salad & jalapeño futomaki
185
tuna salad & sweetcorn
futomaki 185
tuna salad & tomato futomaki
185
tuna salad futomaki 168, 185
tuna salad onigiri 257, 275
tuna salad, red kidney beans &
green pepper futomaki 185
tuna salad with red radish,
cress & onion temaki 245
tuna salad with sweetcorn
temaki 236, 245
tuna sashimi herb ceviche,
shallot & ponzu olive oil 211
tuna & sweetcorn futomaki 173
tuna tataki, spring onion &
wasabi mayo gunkan 113
turbot 85, 116, 121, 190-1, 196
turbot & shiso gunkan 121
turbot ceviche with coriander
& chive gunkan 116
turbot, oroshi daikon white
radish & yubiki nigiri 85
turbot, ume plum & chives
nigiri 79
Umeboshi pickled plum &
cucumber temaki 242
umeboshi pickled plum & shiso
temaki 242
umeboshi pickled plum, daikon
& green bean temaki 242
umeboshi plums 269, 277, 281

ume plum & cucumber
hosomaki 123, 136
ume plum & daikon white
radish hosomaki 136
ume plum & shiso chirashi 269
ume plum & shiso hosomaki
136
ume plum & shiso onigiri 277
ume plum & shiso rice bowl
281
ume plum furikake seasoning
187
ume plum paste 79, 87, 88,
113, 123, 136, 139, 142, 156,
172, 174, 209, 239, 242, 269
umeshu plum wine 182, 271
unagi faux eel kabayaki &
cucumber temaki hand roll
222, 238
unagi faux eel kabayaki
chirashi 270
unagi faux eel kabayaki
dogfish, green beans &
avocado temaki 238
uni sea urchin 218
uni sea urchin & burnt creamy
miso mayo gunkan 105, 118
uni sea urchin gunkan 112
uramaki 24-5
usuzukuri thinly sliced turbot,
ponzu, oroshi daikon & shiso
cress 196, 213

Venison 271
vinegared & wasabi cucumber
pickles 49
vinegared herring sashimi 212
vinegared mackerel pressed
sushi 280
vinegared sardine sashimi 212

Wafu salad dressing 52
wagyu 162
wakame seaweed 27, 30, 202,
218, 248
wasabi mayo 50
wasabi powder 251
whitefish sashimi of red mullet,
leeks & ginger oroshi 190-
1, 210
white tuna sashimi ceviche,
hijiki & truffle olive oil 214
wrasse usuzukuri sashimi 213

Yaki-grilled rice balls onigiri
259, 276
yellowfin tuna, spring onion &
wasabi mayo temaki hand
roll 221, 237
yellowtail see hamachi
yellowtail
yellowtail & shiso gunkan 121
yellowtail tempura hosomaki
135, 143
yellowtail tuna & spicy daikon
futomaki 172
yokan adzuki bean jelly &
chestnut sweet nigiri 91
yokan adzuki bean jelly sweet
nigiri 91
yokan bean paste 91
yuba soy milk skin & wasabi
pressed sushi 279
yuba tofu 176
yubiki scalded red snapper
nigiri 69, 85
yuzukosho 76, 86, 89, 117, 183
yuzukosho paste 143, 166, 237
yuzu mayo 34, 50
yuzu vinaigrette 52